THE AVERAGE INVESTOR'S

RAGE

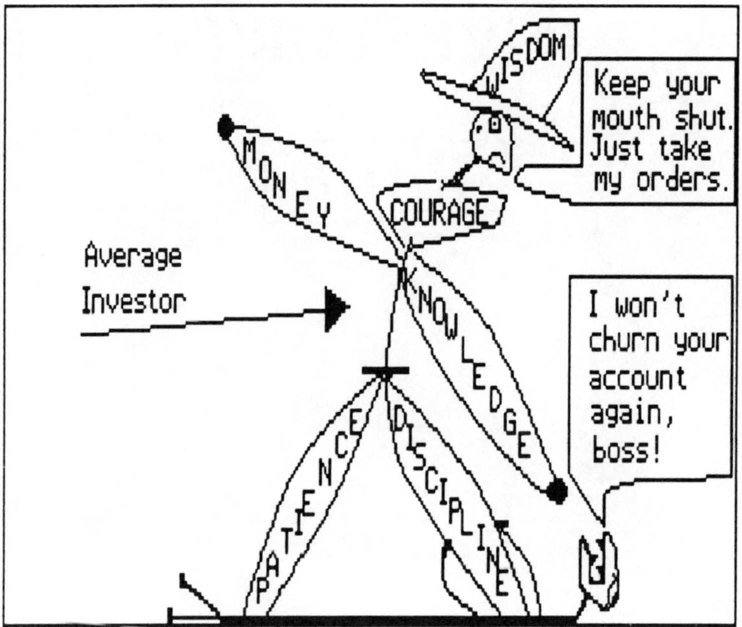

LESSON: The assets necessary to resist fast-talking salespeople.

DEK

THE AVERAGE INVESTOR'S

RAGE

Donald E. Kendrick

VANTAGE PRESS
New York • Los Angeles

FIRST EDITION

Published by Vantage Press, Inc.
516 West 34th Street, New York, New York 10001
Manufactured in the United States of America
ISBN: 0-533-09106-3
Library of Congress Catalog Card No.: 90-90106

To Charmian

For her support and understanding during the difficult task of writing this book.

To Van Mayhall Jr.

For his outstanding legal advice as well as his assistance during my registering as an investment adviser and the writing of this book.

Truth

The greatest homage we can pay to *TRUTH* is to use it.

Emerson

TRUTH is the foundation of all knowledge and the cement of all societies.

Dryden

Contents

LESSON: There is no limit to what some people will do for commissions.

DEK

Introduction

What This Book Is: It is an attempt to demonstrate the dangers you will face in the management of your capital. Remember—"your capital" is "your future" in many respects. How well or how poorly you manage your capital will make a very big difference to you financially, in the years to come. *There are very few industries that can affect your financial life more than the brokerage industry. Unscrupulous stockbrokers can harm you, your family, and your heirs like no other person in your life.*

I do not believe that money is everything—but try living without it and see how great things are! This book will also show you some of the many techniques for investing that have helped me become financially independent.

What This Book Is Not: This book is not an indictment against the brokerage industry. It is an attempt to point out the atrocious conflict of interest that is present when a salesperson is paid a high percentage of a client's commission every time he or she buys or sells. Of course, there are many outstanding men and women in every industry who do outstanding jobs for their clients.

Although my knowledge and expertise involve the brokerage industry, my friends and associates assure me that the basic problem is applicable to salespeople in many other industries.

All opinions expressed in this book are mine. They are based on my personal experiences over twenty years in the financial world—eleven years as a stockbroker. My clients included chairmen of corporations, officers of major corporations, presidents of very large privately held corporations, a member of the Federal Reserve Bank, and, of course, many wealthy individual investors.

I have used sources of information that I believe to be reliable and accurate. Every effort has been made to ensure the accuracy of the information, but where the human element is involved, errors can and do occur. Identities of individuals have not been revealed. Alterations in some of the skits have been made so that no one can be identified personally. The purpose of this book is to make investors aware of the dangers that are present in the investment arena.

There is no intention in this book to single out anyone in particular. Any similarities to anyone you know are purely coincidental.

WHO SHOULD READ THIS BOOK?

All serious-minded investors think they are playing on a level playing field. THEY ARE NOT! All the books in the world on technical analysis or fundamental analysis will do you little good, if you do not realize *there is a much bigger threat to your investment success than the typical market fluctuation.*

Managers of brokerage firms and stockbrokers are between you and most financial vehicles in most cases. If you are not disciplined and careful, you will find you have paid enormous commissions, traded "in and out" a great deal, and stand in pretty bad shape after many years. Even in bull markets, you will find

that all your buying and selling did not do for you what patience and following the trend could have done for you—with fewer commissions.

There are, of course, exceptions to everything. Don't waste your time looking for the exception. Know the danger is there when you deal with a stock salesperson, option salesperson, tax-shelter salesperson, or commodity salesperson. Remember, they are salespeople trying to get commissions to live on. No matter how many fancy titles he or she may have, *BEWARE*—if he or she is paid a percentage of the commissions you pay when you buy or sell. If you laugh at these words, then you have had very few dealings with stockbrokers or similar types. If you have had many years of dealing with stockbrokers, then you may not be laughing because it may be too late for you. But you know I am speaking the truth.

PURPOSE OF THIS BOOK

The first purpose of this book is to truly help you—the average investor. This book will inform you of the conflict of interest that exists when a stockbroker is paid a percentage of the commissions paid by the client. This can encourage overtrading in its many *ugly* forms, thus harming a client, financially. I shall show you how to handle this problem and share with you some of the things that have made me financially independent. One day in the future the method of compensation for stockbrokers will change, because such gross abuses are taking place. Read the *Wall Street Journal* for a year or so. Collect all the articles about fraud, churning, and general abuse of clients by stockbrokers. Then, you will better understand why this book is being written. If you think you can escape the smooth-talking broker who seems to know all the answers to all the questions, then be on your guard. You are *ripe for the bite.*

Discount brokers are going to bring about major changes in the way stockbrokers are paid. If stockbrokers were so smart, then more of their customers would be making fortunes in profits, instead of paying out fortunes in commissions, and making considerably fewer profits for themselves; or even losing money after all the trading has taken place.

Where Are the Customers' Yachts? is the title of a book written in the 1940s. The bankers and stockbrokers had yachts. The naive investor looked around and asked: "Where are the customers' yachts?" "Where is your yacht?" I wonder.

The second purpose of this book is to show you, the average investor, some of the ways you can make better decisions about your investments. You will probably keep more and larger profits, consistently, after reading this book.

The information and graphs used in this book are from sources believed to be reliable. However, such information cannot be guaranteed. Reasonable care has been taken to assure accuracy.

CAVEAT EMPTOR: LET THE BUYER BEWARE

I am not saying that all stockbrokers, commodity brokers, bond brokers, or salespeople in general are crooked. I am saying there are many less than ethical individuals in most walks of life, and you should, at the very least, know some of the dangers. I am trying to demonstrate in this book how some of these individuals play their deadly games with your money and your future—and your children's future. I am trying to show you how *innocent investors can be harmed, permanently;* without really knowing that the danger even exists—until it is too late!

I am saying—based on over twenty years in the markets, eleven years as a stockbroker, that the method of compensation for many stockbrokers creates a definite conflict of interest.

I do not believe that a client's best interest is served when the broker is paid a percent of the commissions that the client pays by buying and selling. There are too many temptations for many brokers to overcome. The bait is too enticing. Management knows about the greed and motivation of human beings.

A LITTLE COURAGE

A great deal of talent is lost in the world for want of a little courage. Every day sends to their graves obscure men whom timidity prevented from making a first effort; who, if they could have been induced to begin, would in all probability have gone great lengths in the career of fame. The fact is that, to do anything in the world worth doing, we must not stand back shivering and thinking of the cold and danger, but jump in and scramble as well as we can.

It will not do to be perpetually calculating risks and adjudging nice chances; it did very well before the Flood, when a man would consult his friends upon an intended publication for 150 years, and live to see his success afterwards; but at present, a man waits, and doubts, and consults his brother, and his particular friends, till one day he is sixty years old and that he has lost so much time in consulting cousins and friends that he has no more time to follow their advice.

Sydney Smith
1771–1845

Foreword

Who is this Donald E. Kendrick? Why does he think we should spend our hard-earned money on his book on investments?

Donald E. Kendrick had served his country in the United States Air Force, obtained an English bride, obtained his college degree and was working as an ambitious stockbroker with one of the largest firms on Wall Street when we first became acquainted through a mutual friend.

I traded a small account with the typical small results, but I felt there was something different about this young man, who had come from a humble background. I wanted to know what was going to happen to him.

Donald has endured financial and personal tragedy that would have destroyed most men. Donald, and his biggest supporter—his lovely wife, Charmian—emerged stronger and more determined than ever to succeed.

After leaving the life of the paid stockbroker, and leaving my account with another broker that did not share the same feeling for my personal success, Donald left the U.S.A. to spend some time in England with his wife and daughter.

Upon Donald's return to the U.S.A. in 1979, he took his life's savings (equity from his home and the money from his wife's furniture), and started to do what he knew best—making money in the market place.

I believe that through long hours of study and years of dedication, Donald E. Kendrick, while young by my standards, has accumulated a data bank of information in his mind that cannot be duplicated. He is dedicated to his plan, and seldom can he be distracted.

One trait that I admire the most in Donald is his desire to help his acquaintances to participate in the market. However, because of their ignorance, there are very few that appreciate the opportunity to draw on his knowledge and experience. Some think that a person who does not get up and go to work at some office outside of their home can't really be legitimate. These qual-

ify as ignorant, and pass up a once in a lifetime opportunity.

Donald E. Kendrick has paid his dues. He has made a lot of money for a "country boy." I am glad he is willing to share some of his knowledge with the world.

I wish my friend, Donald E. Kendrick, much success.

Clement L. Burwell M.B.A., CPA

Preface

Donald E. Kendrick originally became interested in the stock, bond, and commodity markets while in college. He enjoyed trading so much that he decided—with encouragement from his economics professor—to make it his career.

Mr. Kendrick learned very quickly that being a stockbroker is not the same as being a successful investor. Brokerage firms hire young brokers to sell and produce commissions from their clients. Although Mr. Kendrick was quite successful in acquiring large accounts because of his love of the markets, he was never really happy being a salesman—which is all a typical stockbroker is.

After being lulled into thinking that the best way to make money in the stock market was to buy and hold, Mr. Kendrick lost considerable funds; funds he had borrowed to invest in the market. The stock he purchased went from $35 per share to zero and was delisted from the New York Stock Exchange. It took him several years to repay the borrowed money plus interest. This was one of the most important lessons Wall Street taught Mr. Kendrick. At this point he decided to make a change in his career. Although he continued to be a stockbroker for another five years, he was constantly trying to figure a better way to make big money in the marketplace.

In February 1979, Mr. Kendrick finally decided to leave the brokerage business, after eleven years. He moved to England for a year to study the financial markets overseas. While in England, he decided to take all his capital, which amounted to about $70,000 and trade the markets in a manner that he felt would work.

After ten years of trading, Mr. Kendrick is financially independent. However, he is still very unhappy with many of the things that he had to do as a stockbroker to make a living. He decided to write this book in the hope that it will help millions of investors avoid many of the mistakes that he made. He is trying to give back some of the many things he has spent a lifetime learning from so many investors, stockbrokers, and the marketplace.

Mr. Kendrick believes that you will benefit enormously from reading his book. He has taken the time to put his experiences into a form that you can read easily and carry with you. He wishes you every success with your investment goals.

Think for yourself!

THE AVERAGE INVESTOR'S

RAGE

Chapter 1

How Some Stockbrokers Abuse Their Clients—Insight into Why Some Brokers Think as They Do

LETTER TO ALL STOCKBROKERS

Date———

Dear *Stockbroker:*

I have decided to institute new policies and procedures in *(year)* regarding my trading and investment procedures. This letter is to instruct all my stockbrokers to *never call me on the telephone again.* Any correspondence should be made by mail on company letterhead.

When I have orders to give regarding purchases or sales, I shall be precise in my instructions.

I respectfully request that no comments regarding the market, politics, or individual stocks be mentioned.

Simply repeat my instructions to avoid error. Do not even call to report executions. I shall call you.

This should not be construed as criticism of any one person. It is simply my policy decision based on many years of experience. My account is so large that I must establish policies and procedures whereby I have complete control over all external input.

You know, of course, all my orders and positions are to be kept strictly confidential and not discussed or revealed to anyone.

Thank you very much. You will be hearing from me.

Most sincerely,
Your name

TOPICS COVERED IN CHAPTER 1

Have you ever felt like this?
Brokerage offices—key people
Appearance of confidence and knowledge
Pensions of managers
Mistakes of managers
Entering brokerage offices
Insensitive people
The time to avoid trouble with your stockbroker
Wall Street Journal articles on Wall Street abuses

Boardroom sitters
The metamorphosis of a commodity broker turned manager
Stop orders
Options—wasting assets
Death wish of a client
If you refuse to think for yourself
Bust that order
Financial advisory letters
Sophisticated—and stupid
Confessions of some stockbrokers

HAVE YOU EVER FELT LIKE THIS?

I am damned tired of listening to my stockbroker, year after year, and losing money! I am not going to put up with it anymore! I have had enough! Paying out tens of thousands of dollars in commissions, *so the stockbroker can live like a king—at my expense!* If you have felt like this, believe me when I tell you that you are not alone.

Remember, it is not how much you make that makes you independent; *it is how much you accumulate.*

Read this book and *your investment life* will benefit *for the rest of your life.*

BROKERAGE OFFICES—KEY PEOPLE

Most average-size brokerage offices have *two key people:* The *manager* (God, to the brokers under him) and the *largest producer* (stockbroker). These people are *company men!* They are not there to be your friend. They are there to take care of their company and its best interest. They know their *financial future* is secure, for the cream of the accounts coming into the office will go to them; or to someone they want to help in the office, who thinks like they do. This builds *financial loyalty.* It is the old "I scratch your back, you scratch my back" routine. The customers' commissions are their feeding ground.

Managers of stock brokerage offices are not necessarily the most knowledgeable or successful in the marketplace. They are there, usually, because of family connections or because they will run over anybody (you, the client) or young stockbrokers to get to the executive suite. Nepotism is rampant within Wall Street firms. I know for I have seen a great deal of it.

Managers are policemen for the brokerage firms. They are there to protect the firm and its capital. They are not there to make you money. They drive their stockbrokers to "sell, sell, sell." If you, the client, are blind to all this, then, you will pay dearly, especially, if you think a manager is your friend. I shall repeat this many times, because I know most of you do not know or believe what I am saying.

A favorite cliché I have heard about managers who fire stockbrokers for not meeting their quotas (commissions from you) is: "If you put a mule (stockbroker) to the plow and he cannot pull the plow, then you must unhitch (fire) the mule and get another mule." You did know that your stockbroker has a quota to meet? If it is not met, he or she can be terminated—and, often, is terminated!

Most investors do not really think much about the difference between the manager and their stockbroker. Well, there is a huge difference. Since the brokerage industry is run along military lines, you can think of the stockbroker as a private and the manager as a base commander. That is a very big difference, indeed! The manager keeps a low profile in the office. He or she lets the stockbrokers do the mingling with the average client. You will find out who is really the boss when you have a problem; better yet, if you create a problem within the brokerage office. The manager will let you know, promptly—through the broker, usually—that you must not come back in "his or her" office, or some other chastisement, to let you know that your behavior is not acceptable. If the manager calls you on the telephone, then you know you really have transgressed, and he or she may forbid you from entering his or her office again. If you do, he can, indeed, *have you arrested for trespassing.*

If you are losing money because of poor judgment of the stockbroker you are using, forget about getting your money back. The manager usually will suggest that you use another broker in the office. If he or she thinks you are a threat to the office, and the firm, he or she will ban you from coming back into the office. I have seen it happen for the most petty of reasons.

You must understand that you are dealing with these people's livelihoods (your commission dollars), their careers, and their futures. Your future is not really their concern; although they will pretend it is, until you take your commissions elsewhere.

Profits of the brokerage office must be always first. You, the investor, are expendable. Your future does not count for anything. If you get wiped out by overtrading, to generate commissions, then there will be no tears shed for you. The manager will hire "brokers who will do the job." An individual broker may have compassion for an individual investor that he or she gets to know, personally.

However, the manager will have no such compassion. His or her mission is to make sure the office prospers. He or she also gets a piece of the profits.

Stockbrokers come and go. Clients come and go. But the brokerage office will most likely survive over the years, unless the brokers destroy too many investors with their overtrading and high-commission retail offerings. If huge losses occur, then the entire office of brokers, following the manager, will likely contact another brokerage firm. *The manager will negotiate the best deal for himself or herself, and then do what he or she can for his or her troops (stockbrokers). They typically try to stay together because they know that they may hang individually, but, perhaps not, as a group. There is strength in numbers—oftentimes.*

Then, they start all over again; calling on naive investors. This is truly a deadly business that can harm a family financially for generations.

APPEARANCE OF CONFIDENCE AND KNOWLEDGE

Managers are trained to give the appearance of confidence and knowledge. The average investor assumes a manager knows how to make a fortune in the stock market. It is just not true—necessarily. In my twenty years in the financial world, I have personally known quite a few managers of brokerage offices—at least two dozen.

Managers are supervisors of stockbrokers; they are puppets of the higher-up executives within the firm. I heard one manager refer to himself as a "pit boss." If you have ever been to Las Vegas, you know that the pit boss is "the man" at the gambling tables.

If you ever get into financial trouble at a brokerage office, you will find out very quickly what the manager is there for. You will see a side to these individuals that is much different from the one you saw when you were paying thousands of dollars in commissions and "trading your head off—like a drunken sailor." You probably thought you were buying goodwill for the future. Forget it! When your commissions stop, you are no longer any good to them. They will go on to someone else who will pay to learn—as you have.

While sitting in the conference room of a major brokerage office, I overheard the manager discussing a 60 percent payout and a 40 percent payout on different products the broker had sold to a client. I heard the laughter about the "turkey" buying "that stuff," but I did not hear, at any time, about the profits the client had made or was likely to make. I know that the real estate tax shelter being discussed developed a large loss. I have seen oil and gas programs that were really big losers—for the investors, but not for the brokers.

Remember, the payout is the part the broker gets out of the commissions *you* have paid.

PENSIONS OF MANAGERS

Managers realize very early in life that there are only two ways to go in the investment world: (1) Take care of themselves or (2) Take care of clients who are very fickle and come and go. They decide to go with the company all the way.

Mangers are under contract. They receive a much better deal than a stockbroker. They tell the stockbrokers that the real money is made by the stockbrokers. They say that being a manager is the "pits." Can you believe they would say this to reasonably intelligent individuals? Can you believe that some of the stockbrokers believe these lies?

I have known managers and stockbrokers who work long enough to qualify for a pension with one brokerage firm, then move to another firm to start working on another pension. Each time, the pension went to the individual manager or broker; not to the clients who had paid enormous commissions over the years. I am not saying this is wrong. I just doubt that the average investor thinks about the pension he or she is helping to build the manager or broker, *while trading his or her head off.*

In discussing thc contract that one manager I knew was about to sign, he said, "Don, I am not signing my contract until all the 'i's have been dotted and all the 't's have been crossed. I learned a long time ago that you had better get the best deal you can get on the front end, because five years can be a long time." In other words, he is assured of his job for five years. The stockbrokers under him have no such assurance.

MISTAKES OF MANAGERS

Managers make mistakes, just like everyone else in the marketplace. What amazes me is that they can be so *WRONG, WRONG, WRONG, and, yet, because they have a fancy office and title, the average investor thinks that the manager knows more than he or she does. Businessmen, in particular, assume that the manager is very sophisticated because of his or her position. What they do not realize is that most managers* are there because they are *company men,* not soothsayers. Many managers I have known had absolutely awful investment records although they pretend otherwise to their clients. I have seen some of their monthly statements, which is where the truth lies.

One manager I knew made a very large error on an order. If he had been a stockbroker, he would have had to reimburse the company for the loss that he incurred when the error was corrected. This manager, however, simply made the operations manager log the error into the house error account. Only a manager could do that—and get away with it.

ENTERING BROKERAGE OFFICES

If you find that you must go into a brokerage office, do not be intimidated or impressed by the decor of the office, especially if it is a full-service brokerage office. Recognize that investors, just like yourself, have paid dearly for the expensive decor. I would urge you to *avoid going into a brokerage office unless it is absolutely necessary because you become a target* for the hungry young brokers who are constantly looking for new sources of commissions.

Brokerage offices are designed to stimulate trading. The typing of secretaries, squawk boxes with their constant chatter, and the rat-a-tat-tat of the Reuters or Dow-Jones news wires are just some of the trappings of a typical brokerage office. Sometimes an air of urgency is in the air because of some news event. *You must learn to ignore all this.*

Do not think for one minute that these brokers are there to make you rich. *It is their mission to generate commissions . . . from customers' accounts.* You are no exception. These stockbrokers have quotas to meet, just as any salesperson has quotas to meet. In a way, *you are a quota.* A certain number of new accounts are needed by every stockbroker. It is like new blood for a vampire. They have to have new accounts or die—as stockbrokers.

Individual investors come and go, but the broker wants to stay there for his or her *high income from commissions, pension, and the good life.* The broker's family has many needs that require lots of commissions. Remember, a stockbroker is paid 30 percent, 40 percent, or more of every commision dollar you pay. *The more you buy and sell, the more money the stockbroker makes.* So, when you are talking to a stockbroker, recognize that you are the boss. Be demanding! After all, it is your money that is paying the commissions, not the stockbroker's money.

INSENSITIVE PEOPLE

Insensitive people are those who pretend they are considerate, while, all the time, they are taking advantage of everyone around them.

After a stockbroker had recommended that I buy a stock

which subsequently dropped precipitously, I called him and asked, "What should I do with the stock you recommended to me that has dropped 50 percent?" He said, "I don't care what you do with it! *Shove it up your ass, for all I care!"*

That says it all! If it had gone up, he would have bragged about how smart he was. *Don't you see? You cannot come out ahead dealing with people like this.*

THE TIME TO AVOID TROUBLE WITH YOUR STOCKBROKER

Remember that a stockbroker is not *your* stockbroker, but an employee of the brokerage firm that has hired him or her—to sell you something. The time to avoid a problem with a stockbroker is at the very beginning of a relationship. You should be very selective when you decide to do business with a stockbroker. Once you have decided on a particular broker, or several, as the case may be, be extremely specific in what you expect of this person. Negotiate the best commission rate you can. Remember, discount brokers are excellent for those of you who make your own decisions. I encourage you to think for yourself.

Be very demanding and do not tolerate mediocrity or laziness when it comes to the executions of your orders. Let the broker know you are the boss from the beginning. It is your money! If you ever relinquish control, I think you will find your account being abused in short order. Never allow any order to be entered without your approval. Never give total discretion to anyone over your account! A large percentage of legal problems arises from discretionary accounts.

My experience in over twenty years in the marketplace tells me you should keep an arm's length approach with most stockbrokers. Do not try to be friends with them. Keep everything very businesslike. Forget about being a "Mr. Nice Guy!" Remember the old saying: "Nice guys get stepped on."

WALL STREET JOURNAL ARTICLES ON WALL STREET ABUSES

For the sake of brevity, I have listed some of the endless articles on abuses by brokers and member firms that have appeared in the *Wall Street Journal.* If you go to a library that has the *Wall Street Journal* on microfilm, you will find the *Journal,* with these dates, especially interesting. If you take this time to look into this matter, I believe you will benefit enormously.

1. March 22, 1983
2. March 31, 1983
3. March 12, 1984
4. April 26, 1984
5. April 18, 1984
6. May 4, 1984
7. May 10, 1984
8. May 30, 1984
9. June 19, 1984
10. July 6, 1984

11. July 13, 1984
12. July 20, 1984
13. August 7, 1984
14. December 24, 1984
15. May 3, 1985
16. June 13, 1985
17. June 20, 1985
18. August 16, 1985
19. February 25, 1986
20. May 15, 1986

QUESTIONS YOU SHOULD ASK *THE* STOCKBROKER—NOT *YOUR* STOCKBROKER

Look into the eyes of the stockbroker you think you can trust, and ask him or her the following questions:

1. Do you put my best interest first, or do you have a commission in mind first?
2. If I lose all my money by following your advice, will you reimburse me?
3. Are your family and career more important to you than my family and future?
4. What exactly will you do for me if I go bankrupt, following your advice?
5. Can I see your monthly statements for one year—at least—on your own account to see how well you have done? Be adamant about keeping the broker's feet to the fire, so you can flush out the con artist, who is simply trying to churn your account. An honest broker should be happy to show you his or her statements, including the losers.
6. Are you going to give me competitive commission rates? Negotiable items with the stockbroker are:
   a. Margin interest rates (usually a small percent above broker loan rates).
   b. Commission rates (stocks, bonds, commodities) can be negotiated down considerably. I have gotten 70 percent off regular rates from one major brokerage house, and 60 percent off the regular rate at another major house. The commissions were still higher than those charged at the discount house I used. This is quite common, not rare at all. This tells you how ridiculously high the commissions are for someone who just pays the stated rate. "A fool and his money are soon parted—especially on Wall Street."

After you have seen quite a few stockbrokers come and go, you must realize that the brokerage business is not like any other business. The longer it takes you to realize the dangers involved, the more it is likely to cost you.

Never underestimate your enemy! Once you have it straight in your heart and mind, the way it really is, your investment life will take a definite turn for the better.

I THOUGHT I WAS IMMUNE TO THE PITCHES

I thought because I had been a stockbroker for eleven years, I would be immune to the fast-talking salespeople they call stockbrokers. But I found myself being hustled by young brokers who, I thought, would have known better. Besides, I even tried to help

several young brokers by actually trading when I really shouldn't. They would come to my home, borrow my books, and ask questions about the market, the economy, and their future prospects.

To say that I found myself being used by these young "barracudas" is an understatement. One of them even said to me: "Don, why did you think you would be treated any differently, now that you are no longer a stockbroker?" Enough said?

PITTING BROKERS AGAINST EACH OTHER

Managers pit one broker against another in a competitive environment, so that every broker is trying to out-produce the other one. A commission run is often kept in the manager's office so that each broker can see how he or she stands in the office, relative to every other broker. It is strictly a numbers game. I have known managers who hung the daily commission run inside the door of their offices; you could simply stick your head inside the door, and see where you ranked in the office for the day, the week, the month, and the year.

Nowhere have I ever seen the computer run showing the most profitable investor! Never!

The irony is that, when a client gets churned too much, he or she will go to the manager. The manager will encourage the investor to try another broker who is more in tune with the client's needs. What a lot of bull sh—! It is the manger who continues to push the brokers to generate more commissions. After all, the manager is judged by the regional vice-president. The manager's job is to get commissions from his or her brokers' clients. The manager is supposed to create an air of supremacy; of being wise, intelligent, and above the battle. The manager is the driving force behind many brokers getting into trouble by overtrading, no matter what anyone says. And, when the young broker gets into trouble, the manager lets him or her go for the good of the firm. But the manager is still there, and the broker, who is made to look like the villain, is gone. Read the *Wall Street Journal* for a year or two, and see the terrible situations that develop. Thank God for the *Wall Street Journal!*

When a broker has been producing for a while, but is not getting the commissions that the firm believes justifies his or her position, the manager will very quietly let the broker go. The desk and telephone where the broker sat are assigned to another young broker who knows that a specific production quota comes with that desk. If the new broker does not meet the production quotas (commissions), he or she will be gone, also.

CHIP—CAPITAL HAS ITS PRIVILEGES

They say in the military that rank has its privileges—RHIP. Well, *capital has its privileges,* also—*CHIP.* Do not allow your position to be usurped by a salesman or manager who sees you as a "walking commission machine." YOU ARE THE BOSS BECAUSE IT IS YOUR MONEY.

SAYINGS OF STOCKBROKERS I HAVE KNOWN

1. If you are going to recommend, recommend often.
2. You have to boil the hog to get the fat: hog = customer, fat = commissions
3. You can't cook an omelet without breaking some eggs: eggs = customer, omelet = commissions
4. Hold still little fish, while I gut you!
5. I know you have a loss, but I have lost more; *a lie!*
6. I just bought some, and I want you to *buy* some, too. The *stockbroker bought one share.*
7. I have some good inside information, but keep it a secret. Buy quick.
8. Use stop orders (great commission generators).
9. *Buy* some options . . . puts—calls . . . something! (Constant turnover—options are paid in cash so there is no risk to the brokerage firm.)
10. *Sell* some options for income against your stocks. (Great commissions, also, if the stock is called.)
11. Earnings are up; better *buy* quick!
12. Earnings are down; better *sell* quick!
13. Dividend increased; better *buy* quick!
14. Dividend cut; better *sell* quick!
15. New product will revolutionize *whatever. Buy!*
16. Technical support. *Buy!*
17. Fundamentals look great! *Buy.*
18. Fundamentals look terrible! *Sell.*
19. P/E ratio too high! *Sell.*
20. P/E ratio too low! *Buy.*
21. Moving-average line turning up/down. *Buy/Sell.*
22. Prime rate increased/decreased. (Up is bad, down is good.) *Sell/Buy.*
23. Cycle too high/low. *Sell/Buy.*
24. Too late to sell, too early to buy—*put spreads on.*
25. Major news event: President has heart attack. *Sell.*
26. Just trust me!
27. More bang for your buck—commodities, options, margin.
28. Your stock is boring, boring, boring! (Used to persuade client

to *sell* and *buy* something else [this generates more commissions].)

29. Your stock is so slow, it is like watching paint dry.
30. Lions-4, Christians-0—A favorite phrase of a stockbroker I once knew.

SWINDLE THE SUCKERS

After a long conversation with a senior stockbroker who was with a leading brokerage firm, he said, "Let me go; I've got to 'swindle' some more suckers out of some commissions before the market closes."

My question to you is: "Are you going to allow this to happen to you?" If you do, you will pay a dear price; and so will your family.

THE PERFECT INVESTMENT

A quick way to determine if stockbrokers do, indeed, put your best interest first is to imagine there was one stock, or no-load mutual fund that would serve your investment needs for the rest of your life. You would never have to make another decision again. Do you think your stockbroker would tell you about it? *Think about it.* You would never pay another commission!

YOU MUST TRADE SOME TO JUSTIFY A DISCOUNT

When your full-service stockbroker says you have to trade in order to earn a discount, tell him—*NO!* None of your first-class discount brokers makes you trade a lot before you get a discount. You get a discount from the first trade—and rightly so. Do not throw your money away trying to impress someone who is only trying to get his or her hand into your pocket.

NO! NO! NO!

This is the most powerful word in the English language. If you have trouble saying, No, to a stockbroker or salesman, just say, "I'll have to discuss this with my wife/husband. I'll get back to you if I'm interested." YOU MUST LEARN TO SAY: NO-NO-NO!

LOSSES, LOSSES, EVERYWHERE

See what your stockbroker has to say, when you are looking at huge losses from his or her recommendations. It is lonely at the top, I have heard it said. Well, believe me, it is horrible at the bottom of a decline, with huge losses—and no cash. *Worse yet is to be sold out, as a result of margin calls, at the bottom in the midst of a panic.*

RELIGIOUS STOCKBROKERS

While I was residing in England, a manager and producing stockbroker in the United States contacted me about handling some of my business. He was with a major Wall Street firm on the east coast. During our conversation on the telephone, he kept saying how our relationship as Christians was the really important thing. I told him I would need a competitive commission rate. He said, "Sure, sure!" He sent me the forms for stocks, options, commodities—the whole ball of wax. He called several times to see where the forms were. Finally, I decided to do about one-third of my busines with him, under the right circumstances. *I never do all my business with one firm.* I like to spread it out so that no one knows all my positions. You should consider this as your account grows.

In any case, after I sent the forms with my stiff requirements for discounts, which I was getting at several other brokerage firms, I never heard from him again. I don't suppose he cared as much about our "Christian relationship" as he said, after all.

I have seen and heard about everything you can imagine by stockbrokers. Please remember, if there is a way to separate you from your money, someone is awake at night trying to figure out how.

DRUGS ON WALL STREET

You should also realize that drugs and alcohol are often used by some stockbrokers. Therefore, any advice you receive should be obtained in writing on the company letterhead. I was approached once, by a very successful stockbroker, in a very wealthy part of the United States. He asked me if I wanted to make "some really big money!" I asked if it was legal. He said: "Does that really matter?" I said, "You bet your ass it matters." He said he would come over to my home and discuss it further with me. I told him, if it was illegal, to forget it!

I was driving to work a few days later, and I heard about this *huge drug bust*. Then I heard the young broker's name on the radio as one of those caught. I almost lost control of my car. Who knows how close I came to being implicated with him? He was handsome, well liked, and had a bright future. But it wasn't enough, apparently.

I was told, several years later, that this young broker had killed himself. What a waste! Still, you, the average investor, must know that stockbrokers are human beings. Do not be so quick to turn over your financial future to stockbrokers in the future.

EXPENSIVE CLOTHES—GLASSES, SHOES, AND A FANCY CAR

Do not let expensive clothes lead you to think that the broker who dresses expensively is any wiser or smarter than you are. This is an old ploy by salespeople of this ilk. It is sad to say that too many investors are impressed with expensive clothes, sophisticated-looking eyeglasses, silver hair, and expensive shoes. Likewise, fancy or expensive automobiles and homes are also trappings that many supersalespeople use to convey to their prospects that they are successful. Beware of the expensive trappings and the superficial allurements. You could be falling for the trap, like so many have before you.

If you allow a stockbroker to churn your account (trade excessively for the purpose of generating commissions with no regard for the objectives of the client) and you lose considerably, you can forget recovering everything you lost. It is acknowledged around Wall Street that "what is theirs is theirs; what is yours is negotiable." That means that, as long as you keep control of your money, it is yours. Once you pay it out in commissions, it is no longer yours; it is their money (commissions), and they will fight to keep it.

Under a recent Supreme Court ruling, you cannot sue your broker. You must submit to binding arbitration when you feel your stockbroker has fraudulently mishandled your account. You are deprived of your day in court. When you have the Supreme Court of the United States on your side, you have real power, almost total power.

If you sign the binding arbitration agreement, you are bound by it. If you do not sign the form, it is my understanding that you can sue your broker if, indeed, there is fraud. Of course, the brokerage firm is unlikely to open an account for you if you do not sign the form.

APPEALING TO THE CONSCIENCE OF A STOCKBROKER

Forget about appealing to the conscience of a stockbroker. He or she has a manager breathing down his or her neck for more commissions (production). It does not matter whether you win or lose. They just want you to play the game by buying and selling.

You must keep your mind straight. You must understand that some of the leaders in high-finance areas try to keep the masses in the dark.

No matter what you hear, remember that your money is your money. Do not trust the fancy-dressed, button-downed-collar executive with your money. No one has the right to tell you what to do. If you sign away your right to decide, to these money-hungry, career-minded individuals, you will get just what you deserve. I have known many of these individuals. I have often heard the average investor referred to as a "turkey" who needs someone to tell him or her what to do.

COLLEGES AND UNIVERSITIES

Stockbrokers and managers also use some of the college and university campuses for their feeding grounds. *Continuing education* is the department in which you find many stockbrokers teaching young and old about the stock market. They teach how to trade options, stocks, commodities, and the many other areas of financial interest. They seldom, if ever, mention the fact that

commissions are what these stockbrokers are really after.

The universities should not allow instructors to teach naive individuals about investments when the instructors' conflict of interest is so great. Again, *would you put a fox in charge of your henhouse?*

THE AVERAGE INVESTOR'S PROFIT

I have never seen a chart of the profits of the investor anywhere in the brokerage offices in which I have worked or visited. I have seen the commissions of each broker, but never a report of how well the investor is doing. You must realize that the brokerage firm does not survive on your profitability. You could, theoretically, make millions on your investments, but, if you do not buy and sell and pay commissions, the stockbroker gets nothing. How long do you think a stockbroker will be around if he does not persuade you, or someone, to buy or sell something? Not very long, I can assure you.

FOLLOW THE LEADER—BUT WHO LEADS?

Stock analysts are famous for following trends—and each other. When the market is declining, it seems that it will decline forever. No one seems to want to be the first one to acknowledge a change in direction. Just as analysts can be excessively bearish, they can become equally enthusiastic on the bullish side—after the trend is obvious.

The point that seems most important here is that I do not believe most investors are going to make a great deal of money depending on these Johnny-come-lately individuals. You must do your own thinking and recognize the important changes developing, before the masses do. This will, of course, involve being a little early. Still, I have never known anyone who made big dollars by getting in on the exact low or selling out on the exact high. In this business, you can become rich if you come in close to the extreme points and exercise patience enough for ten men!

Learning to stay out of the stock market altogether is another requirement for success in building your fortune. Staying in the market all the time, if the trend is up, works well, but that is rarely the case. The market is famous for discounting recessions that do not occur. However, if your net worth in the market drops by 50 percent or so, you will not care whether the recession occurred or not, for you have a depression of 50 percent. Psychologically, you will find it really drains your mental energy.

SUPEREGOS

Stockbrokers with superegos can break you. They can sound so sure that they can persuade you to invest more than you should in a "sure thing." Of course, if they are wrong, they still have the commissions you have paid them, and you suffer the loss.

They will have another idea waiting in the wings of their minds to make your money back for you. If that idea also fails, they have received another commission, and you have another loss. "But losses are tax deductible," they are quick to point out.

When you finally get burned out, they will just move on to someone else that can pay them their commissions. They usually have a living to make, and a family to support. They cannot allow themselves to get bogged down with your petty problems; such as going bankrupt, because you believed what they said and followed their guidance. After all, you thought these stockbrokers really knew more than you did—about how to invest your money. Perhaps, now you know better. I hope it has not cost you too much.

As a very close friend of mine said, after a Texas stockbroker had really hurt him: "He touched me! Yes, that is what he did! He touched me for a bundle! *I had my eyes open, but my brain was disengaged.*" The interesting point is that he would not admit to me just how much he had really lost.

GRADES IN SCHOOL ARE MUCH LIKE STOCK MARKET PROFITS

Stock market profits are much like grades in school. It takes a lot to get them up, but very little to knock them down. It takes a great deal of buying to put the price of a stock up, but a lack of buyers, and just a little panicky selling, will drive a stock down—sharply.

Ignorance is a terrible blight on humanity. To be ignorant to the ways of stockbrokers and managers is to jeopardize everything that is near and dear to you. Why? Because you are involved with your money; possibly, your entire retirement capital.

When you are old and gray, and it is too late for you to recover your losses, you might remember my words. Learn now, if it is not already too late for you.

MARGIN ACCOUNTS—BUYING WITH BORROWED MONEY

If you borrow money with which to speculate, remember that *you must pay the money back—with interest.* I am assuming that you are honest and intend to pay your debts. This book is not addressed to frauds and cheats. *I have made my money in the market, honestly. You can, also, if you work at it—and persevere—and if you have capital, knowledge, and enough time.* This book should help you avoid many of the pitfalls I did not even know existed—until I fell into them.

Heavy users of margin are rarely long-term investors. The financial cemetery is full of margin traders. Cash buyers can afford to ride the ups and downs out. Margin traders can be wiped out in a sharp decline, if they are overmargined.

Know who, and what, you are before you enter this arena. No mercy will be shown to you if you get in over your head. The worst possible time to make a decision is when you have a margin call. Remember, a margin clerk does not care about P/E ratios, book values, or anything else. You must maintain a certain equity level or they will sell you out to protect the capital of the brokerage firm.

When you borrow money, the interest charges start running from the first day. If you speculate with borrowed money, you must plan on making more on your speculation than the interest costs. I use the word *speculation* more than most because I view most purchases of stock as a speculation of some kind, especially if you are borrowing money to make the purchase. You are less likely to get into serious trouble borrowing money if you approach the thing you are buying as a speculation. Stocks, commodities, and real estate are all speculations. Do not allow some salesperson to lull you into thinking you cannot lose! It happens all the time, whether you hear about it or not. If you do not believe me, take a little time off from your job, and go to the bankruptcy courts.

Stockbrokers, like bankers, make it sound so easy to make money, when you are borrowing the money. But watch how their attitude changes when you get into financial trouble. Then they

remind you of their obligations to their firm or to their depositors. When they ask for more collateral, remember how easy it was to borrow the money. I am speaking from experience.

If you get into trouble, and cannot put up more collateral in a declining situation, the brokerage firms have the authority to sell enough of your assets to protect their assets. You gave them that right when you signed the margin-account agreement form.

They are going to protect their assets first. You are not important, when it comes to their survival. Most people do not sell out of margin accounts until they are forced to sell. The average investor does not reduce his or her debt until forced to. The reason is that most investors have been taught to incur debt and pay back with cheaper dollars. This does not work in the market because of forced liquidations by member firms required by the Federal Reserve Bank Act. The Federal Reserve requirements must be strictly adhered to. A Fed margin call must be met or satisfied with either cash or collateral.

I have heard customers say, as they opened margin accounts: "I am going into this with my eyes open." I have seen them leave with their "financial eyes" closed—permanently. "I just never believed a stock could go that low—that fast!" I have heard many investors say this, or similar statements, over the last twenty years or so.

Stockbrokers tend to sluff off the dangers of a margin account because the account will generate more commissions, usually, than a cash account. Also, some firms—including some of the largest—are now paying the broker part of the interest that you, the client, are paying in interest costs to borrow money from the brokerage firm. So, *the broker wins on commissions and interest charges.*

CRYING TIME IN YOUR LIFE

Have you had your son or daughter look into your eyes and ask: "Mom, Dad, why can't I go to college like my friends? Is it because you lost so much in the stock market and commodity market? Is it true that your stockbroker churned your account so much, buying and selling, that you lost our college money? If so, why did you let that happen?

"Because you lost my college money, I am going to suffer for the rest of my life; my children—your grandchildren—will suffer also. Was the thrill of buying and selling worth our future?"

What I have found so amazing is that the average investor believes whatever a stockbroker tells him or her. The investor doesn't even stop to ask why the broker is stuffing money into his or her pocket. As if money comes that easy!

I still get sick just thinking about the poor, unsuspecting client who just wants a fair shake.

How Wall Street keeps the average investor in the dark is beyond me.

HOW MUCH TIME DO YOU HAVE TO MAKE IT IN THE STOCK MARKET?

Investors think they have all the time in the world to "make it" in the stock market. They do not! You do not either! Bull markets do not last forever. Sometimes it can be many years between the "top of a bull" and the "bottom of a bear" market.

Many investors think that they can be pals with their stockbroker and this will help them. You do not have time to "play at the market." We all get old and we all die. Your children look to you for guidance and support. Do you think, for one minute, that your stockbroker is going to shoulder that responsibility? How about your retirement? Your stockbroker is not going to provide you with that, either. If you allow him or her to churn your account for commissions during your working years, you will wake up one day and find that your stockbroker has retired on your commissions. You may have made a little, a lot, or lost everything, but do not expect your broker to feel sorry for you. You have been a fool! I know! I was one for too many years!

PLATITUDES

Platitudes are typical from your average stockbroker. Trite sayings are little consolation to you, once you have overtraded your account, with the stockbroker getting all the commissions and your sitting with losses. The broker will simply go on to other accounts, in a constant search for more and more commissions, *like a shark that must swim all its life,* without stopping, so *a stockbroker must generate commissions all his or her life, or die, as a stockbroker.* Stockbrokers are paid to sell. They are not paid to let you sit in certificates of deposit or cash equivalents all your investment life. No commissions, no pay is the story I have heard so many times as a stockbroker—from the manager!

BORING—BORING—BORING

If you have a large stock position, and the stock is in your brokerage account, where the stockbroker can watch it every day, Beware! This is a prime target, because it represents a big commission, if the stockbroker can get you to sell it and then reinvest the proceeds on something else. Ergo! Double Commissions.

I had a position of some forty thousand shares of U.S. Industries at one time and the stock was selling at $15 per share. I had told the stockbroker to forget it was there. However, I cannot tell you how many times he would mention something about it.

Finally, I told him to "deliver out all my stocks." This way I would have my stock in my lockbox, and the broker could not watch my position anymore.

I urge you to do likewise. Deliver out your stock and bond positions. This way your investments will not appear on the monthly statements of the brokerage firm. The stockbroker will not be as likely to call you every five minutes.

If the stock you own is inactive, stockbrokers will use phrases like: "Boring, boring, boring!" Other phrases are: "Watching your stock is like watching grass grow," or "Man, this is like watching paint dry."

All of these techniques are designed to persuade you that you have a "dog," and you should sell it. However, if you know the company, and the stock is undervalued and has a good future—just sit tight! Your day will come, for the stock market will seldom let a real value stay that way forever.

Oh, yes, I made over $100,000 on the stock that was so boring. You have to remember, stockbrokers make nothing unless you buy or sell something; activity is necessary for their existence.

NOT EVEN DRY BEHIND THE EARS

Young stockbrokers I have known find it very amusing that older investors will take their advice when they are not even "dry behind the ears." To seriously advise an elderly individual how to invest the precious money he or she has spent his or her life accumulating is an awesome burden. A young broker who does not even know what it means to work for a living should not be put into that position. The image of the all-knowing stockbroker is such a fallacy. I still find it hard to believe that so many investors believe it.

HOLD STILL, LITTLE FISH—WHILE I GUT YOU

This is a phrase that I am reminded of when I see an uninformed investor come into a brokerage office. If you trust the stockbroker to watch out for your best interest, you are running

a grave (like buried) risk. The stockbroker is a salesperson with quotas to meet. He or she is trying to please his or her manager, provide for his or her family and take care of his or her retirement—all out of the commissions you, and others like yourself, pay every time you buy or sell something.

LAUGHING STOCKBROKERS AND CLIENTS

I have seen many laughing investors end up with tears in their eyes. Do not get caught up in the laughter associated with rising markets, only to cry when the bottom falls out of prices. Investors will gladly buy when prices are rising, but sell out when the stocks are truly undervalued.

A wise, old broker called to sell me some stock in a new offering. I told him to show me where he had bought some of this stock, and I would surely buy as much as he did, share for share. He said, *"Don, dear boy, this stuff is for other people's money, not my money—dear boy!"* Enough said?

INTIMIDATION BY STOCKBROKERS

Do not be intimidated by a stockbroker. Remember, it is your money. *You are paying the commissions.* The broker is not doing you a favor talking to you. If he or she thinks so, get another broker. Let him or her know that you expect your best interest to be served; not the broker's. Keep everything on a business

basis and you will do fine. Most average investors get into trouble when they expect something for nothing. There are *no* free lunches—especially in the brokerage business. You are better off if you avoid doing business with relatives and friends. I have tried both ways. *A friend is an enemy whom you cannot see! My best service and business experiences have come from strangers who appreciated my business.*

COMMISSIONS—QUOTES FROM FAMOUS AUTHORS

1. Mr. Darvas described how commissions can harm your capital when overtrading as "commission mice would nibble away at each operation and would finally eat up my capital." (Nicolas Darvas, *How I Made $2,000,000 in the Stock Market,* p. 57)

2. The trader must look far ahead, but the broker is concerned with getting commissions now; hence, the inescapable fallacy of the average market letter. Brokers make their living out of commissions from the public. (Edwin Lefevre, *Reminiscences of a Stock Operator,* p. 34)*

3. Had the broker told it like it really is, he would have said something like: "The name of the game is making money and there isn't one broker worth his salt on Wall Street who doesn't know that the sure way to do that is to stimulate trading because that generates commissions." (William X. Scheinman, *Why Most Investors Are Mostly Wrong Most of the Time,* p. 34) **

4. This is the easiest kind of business to get, and it shows both the highest rate of commissions and client turnover. Moreover, speculators are usually nonmember traders, so the business is done at full commissions.

Also, the firm can generate additional income by putting its clients' excess nonregulated funds into treasuries. And on some

*Reprinted by permission of the publisher, Fraser Publishing Company, Burlington, Vermont 05402.

**Reprinted by permission of the publisher, Traders Press, Inc., Greenville, S.C. 29603.

exchanges it can even post these treasuries as original margin. (Stanley Kroll, *The Professional Commodity Trader,* p.88)*

5. Keep in mind that brokers sometimes innocently become the undoing of many speculators. Brokers are in the business to make commissions. They cannot make commissions unless customers trade. The more trade, the more commissions. The speculator wants to trade and the broker not only is willing but too often encourages overtrading. The uninformed speculator regards the broker as his friend and is soon overtrading. (Jesse Livermore, *How to Trade in Stocks,* p.42)

6. Most brokers live off commissions. For the average brokerage house, tips become a form of chain advertising. A good flow of tips is considered good merchandising. Tip-seekers and

*Reprinted by permission of the publisher, Traders Press, Inc., Greenville, S.C. 29603.

tip-takers are invariably tip-passers. Tip-broadcasting becomes an endless chain. Tip-takers are slaves to habit. They have difficulty resisting the raving and look forward to those tips indispensable to their happiness. (Roy W. Longstreet, *Viewpoints of a Commodity Trader*, p. 53)*

7. In other cases, brokers are finding uncertain trades to keep their clients' money working and, I am sure, to keep the commissions rolling in. (Roy W. Longstreet, *Viewpoints of a Commodity Trader* p.55)*

8. Brokers are paid for the commissions they generate, not for the performance of their clients' accounts. They may look successful, but Gucci shoes, Polo suits, and Pierre Cardin ties have far more to do with good merchandising than with ability in the marketplace. (David Dreman, *Contrarian Investment Strategy*, p. 186)**

THE PAYOUT

You must understand how a stockbroker is paid, if you are to understand why they do some of the things they do. One day, in the future, they may be paid like bank clerks or other order-takers. However, until such time, it is in your best interest to know how a stockbroker is paid.

Stockbrokers are not paid a salary, generally—regardless of what many of them might say. They are paid a draw against commissions, which they are expected to get from you. A general rule of thumb is 30 percent of every commission dollar is paid to the stockbroker. The more commissions the broker gets from you (buying and selling), the higher the percentage of payout to the broker. This is known as the "PC" within the industry. A rough guide of how their pay works is as follows:

0–$50,000	in commissions per year	30% to 35%
$50,000–$100,000	in commissions per year	35% to 42%
$100,000–$150,000	in commissions per year	42% to 45%
$150,000 plus	in commissions per year	45% to 50%

On top of this, there is usually an expense account after reaching a certain level. The expense account is increased as the commissions increase. This does not include stock options, which enable the stockbroker to buy the company's stock below the market price. This also does not include the broker's payout on any margin interest you may pay as a result of trading in a margin account.

The payout (commissions) of public tax-shelter programs is enormous. Fifty percent is common. That means that if you, the client, invested $100,000 in a tax-shelter program of some kind, about $8,500 to $10,000.00 would consist of commissions, depending on whether it was 8½ percent to 10 percent commission charged. The stockbroker on a 50 percent payout would get half of that amount for his or her share and the firm would keep the rest. This should give you some idea of how hopeless your chances are of making any really big money in this type of public offering.

It is almost impossible to make much out of an investment when the salesperson is paid so much out of your capital. One way or the other, that is the only way; no matter what anyone tells you to the contrary.

Now, do you think for one minute that the commissions are not an inducement for the stockbroker to encourage activity (buying and selling) in a client's account? You may think that the broker really cares about your best interest. Look around you; add up your commissions from your activity for the last five years, and ask yourself, honestly: Would you have been better off to just hold your quality stocks in an uptrend, or do all the buying and selling that you have done? Think about it!

SOME OF THE MANY DIFFERENT TYPES OF STOCKBROKERS

1. The young, aggressive type: He or she has all the answers to all the questions, or so he or she pretends. He or she is climbing the "ladder of success." Often, this climb involves climbing over the backs of honest and trusting clients. As one young broker, fresh from his firm's training school said: "I

know I am going to hurt a lot of investors with too many commissions—but I am going to make it in this business." I asked him if he managed to save his soul? "Hell no," he said, "that's the first thing they made us throw out the window." This is why a young stockbroker can be so dangerous. He or she has a stiff commission quota to meet, or get out of the business. Brokerage firms want to drive these young people. Every time one drops by the wayside, the firm keeps a few of the many accounts that the broker has opened, with none of the liabilities that come from an employee who hangs around for a pension. The manager gets the pick of the quality accounts this young stockbroker has brought into the office. This is why a manager ends up with the largest and best-quality accounts over time. These points are so important they are worth repeating time and again. Perhaps, *these words will save you many heartaches and disappointments that so many have suffered because they did not know and there was no book like this to tell it "like it really is."*

2. The middle-aged broker: The middle-aged broker is from the right family ties. He or she belongs to the local country club and follows his or her firm's recommendations right down to the shoelaces. His or her clients may make or lose money, but this broker will never get in too much trouble, following the company's recommendations. If you expect to get rich in the market, this is not the person with whom you should do business.

3. The older, mature type: He or she appears full of wisdom and experience. He or she may be very wise and have a deep insight into the market. Then, again, this broker may be none of these; he or she may be fat, dumb, and lazy. I have seen many of these types within the brokerage business.

4. The retired military officer: The military types usually do pretty well in the brokerage business. They aren't "barn burners," but they follow the corporate line. They take orders without question. The brokerage business is much like the military. There is a definite chain of command. Military men will not rock the boat, usually. *They are not going to risk their neck for you.* They have their military pension and they will get a pension from their brokerage firm. This, plus their Social Security, and

they will have a fine retirement, plus the life they are living isn't too shabby. Therefore, if you are looking for unique, original ideas, do not come to these fellows.

5. The specialist: This individual handles a specific category of investments—mutual funds, life insurance, and so on. He or she gets overrides from all the other brokers who do that kind of business, because he or she is the in-house expert. Some call him or her the coordinator. This broker is there to make a lot of money. He or she is going to "push" the company's products and is not there to help you get rich, either. He or she is also a salesperson.

6. The famous athlete whom everyone knows. Former football,

baseball, and basketball players and other popular athletes are famous for getting into the brokerage business. People like to do business with these individuals just so they can say to their friends "old so-and-so is my broker." Little do they realize how much they pay for that luxury.

LEGEND IN HIS OR HER OWN TIME

Beware of stockbrokers who tell you about an analyst who is a "legend in his or her own time." I have seen more than one "Roman candle"—a shining star for awhile, who then wipes out huge numbers of investors. The average investor is not equipped to match wits with stockbrokers who are trained to sell you something and get that commission.

EIGHTY-YEAR-OLD MAN CRYING

I walked into the men's room one afternoon after a rough day of trading soybeans. An old man whom I had seen in the office a number of times was leaning over the sink. He was crying like a baby. He was wiping his bloodshot eyes with a handkerchief that had seen better days. His hands were shaking something awful. I said, "What's the problem, old-timer?" He said, "Your manager just sold my stocks to meet a margin call. I did not know that he could do that so quickly. Now, I'm broke! Eighty years old—and broke!"

This man should have known better at eighty years of age. He learned the hard way! But too late! When a big break in the market comes, be aware that margin calls can turn into an avalanche of selling.

JUICE = COMMISSIONS

There are those who will disagree with what you are about to read. They will call it sour grapes. *You* just remember what happens when grapes (you) are turned into wine (commissions).

The grapes are crushed. If you want to continue to be crushed, then read no further. I beg of you: Do not be one of the crushed investors because of unscrupulous stockbrokers and managers who allow churning to take place in order to get your juice (commissions). In fact, *commissions are referred to as "juice" by many stockbrokers. Juice is usually obtained by crushing something.*

IGNORANCE OF THE LAW

There is a difference between making and keeping. In the stockmarket, personality means nothing. *Knowledge, money, and*

courage are everything in the marketplace. A sense of history is vital for success. Ignorance of the law is no excuse in a court of law. Likewise, ignorance of the rules of Wall Street will not remove the losses from your account, once they have occurred.

In *Reminiscences of a Stock Operator* on page 151, you find the statement: "You can never bank on there being but one remarkable salesman in the world or on complete immunization from the influence of personality." This statement was true sixty years ago; it is still true today.

Many investors think that their stockbroker is really trying to make them money. Perhaps he or she is. But only in the sense that he or she is getting a commission every time you buy or sell something. When he or she loses you money, what does he or she say? Some of the popular phrases are "Sorry about that." "We'll do better the next time." "Wait until next year; we'll show them,"—with your money, that is. "Well, gee whiz, I lost on that one, too!" "It's been rough all over; everybody is losing." *The excuses go on and on!*

YOUR EARS ARE YOUR ENEMY

1. "Good information seldom comes by way of the ear. . . . Good information needs to be seen. One should question the source of any information that comes by way of the ear." (Roy W. Longstreet, *Viewpoints of a Commodity Trader,* p. 114)*
2. "My ears were my enemy," said Mr. Darvas. (Nicolas Darvas, *How I Made $2,000,000 in the Stock Market,* p. 116)

These quotes are from men who have made fortunes in the real world of investing and trading. The statements are well worth remembering.

THE BOY FROM NEW YORK

A young technical analysist from New York came to a brokerage office in which I worked many years ago. Older, mature investors, who should have known better, gathered around this young man while he looked at a tiny chart book, with, perhaps,

*Reprinted by permission of the publisher, Traders Press, Inc., Greenville, S.C. 29603.

a thousand charts of individual stocks in it. These investors were taking action on their portfolios (that's your list of securities you own), as though his words were coming from on High.

After the investors had left the meeting, there was much laughter among the brokers over the fact that these investors were making serious investment decisions based on what a young man, with a chart book, was telling them. "People want to be led—even if it is over a cliff."

FREE ADVICE FROM FULL-COMMISSION BROKERS

Investors who think they are getting free advice from their stockbroker had better look at their commission charges. The idea of something for nothing is part of the trouble that the average investor has.

Most investors I have known were pretty nice people. They are honest, hardworking individuals who are too busy with their careers to realize how much they can lose through abuses by stockbrokers. They believe they are being treated fairly by their stockbroker. Yes, your securities are safer, and insured for more than ever before. That is not where the real danger lies for the average investor.

The real danger lies in your trusting someone with your financial future when he or she is compensated by the commissions you pay him or her. Whether you are profitable hasn't a thing to

LESSON: Every month a stockbroker starts from zero - for pay purposes. DEK

do with the stockbroker. If you never buy or sell anything, he or she does not get paid—for very long.

Stop and think for a minute. If a stockbroker's clients do not buy or sell something, he or she will not be paid. How long do you think he or she is going to sit there, if he or she is not paid? So, the broker either persuades you to buy or sell something, and often, or he or she is on the street looking for another job. What would you do, if you were in the broker's place, and he or she was in yours? Think about it!

A STOCKBROKER'S BOOK

A stockbroker's book is simply his or her record of each customer, the address and other pertinent information. The client's positions are also included on this record or page. The stocks, bonds, options, and anything else the client might own are listed here. The investment objectives should also be listed to remind the broker, technically, of the client's goals. This is supposed to guide the broker in the types of investments he or she should show the client. Forget it! After a little while, you will be hearing your broker suggest many different investment vehicles; especially, those with high-commission payouts. The broker's book of accounts grows, if he or she is good at selling, and a major bear market does not come along and wipe the clients out. As this book of accounts gets larger and larger, the stockbroker obtains more and more leverage. He or she can become more demanding of the manager because the manager knows that people prefer to do business with individuals with whom they are familiar.

You may think a customer will leave a stockbroker if the broker does not make the client money. It is not necessarily so. It may be true that you would change brokers, but I think *most people fear change more than losses.* Besides, most people feel they may exchange one stockbroker for a worse one. "The devil we know is better than the devil we do not know" is a phrase I have heard often. And, never forget, *most people do not blame their stockbroker, even when the broker is the cause of the losses. Why? Because they would be admitting that they had been very foolish.* How many of you want to admit to yourself, or to your spouse, that your stockbroker or other trusted confidant has been taking advantage of you for many years? Not many of you, I'll wager.

PATIENCE—AN ASSET OR A LIABILITY

Patience on Wall Street can be an asset. However, patience should not be confused with a lack of, or inability to make a decision. Patience to hold a stock or commodity in an uptrend with improving fundamentals is not the same as holding a stock or commodity in a downtrend with deteriorating fundamentals. To never give up does not mean staying with a sinking ship.

THE BROKER'S PRIVATE OFFICE

Brokerage firms capitalize on the instinct (competitiveness) to beat your opponent. They create competition between brokers to generate more and more commissions. This is how many investors get hurt; overzealous salespeople (stockbrokers are salespeople). Many firms use private offices as a perk. The open-floor arena, where the lesser producers sit, is much like a typing pool for large numbers of secretaries. The private offices are reserved for the "big producers." This is the old "carrot and stick" game, again. Nothing can motivate a stockbroker to generate more commissions quicker than the idea that one of those private offices can be his or hers. More commissions are all that are needed, and you know who pays the commissions, don't you?

LIES, LIES, AND MORE LIES

Realize that lies come from all corners of life. Politicians lie, stockbrokers lie, insurance salespeople lie, real estate salespeople lie, preachers lie—and on and on. I am not saying that everyone in these professions lies all the time. However, in my many years of doing business with all kinds of individuals, I have documented so many lies in my diaries that it began to amaze me that individuals you would have thought could be trusted would lie and think nothing of it.

When the kids need shoes, the mortgage needs to be paid, and the car note is past due, who do you think you can trust with your financial future? Think about it!

CONFIDENTIALITY

Don't believe it, if you think your business with your broker is kept confidential. I have had stockbrokers discuss their clients' positions with me, as freely as you would talk about the weather. I have had friends of mine relate how a stockbroker I referred them to would tell my friends what I was buying and selling.

They say there is "honor among thieves." Well, do not believe it, when it comes to stockbrokers. Their business is sell, or get out. There is no time for "Mr. Nice Guys." The manager is there to see that the stockbrokers produce commissions, not to act in the investor's best interest. It would be better for you to make your own decisions and use a discount broker, if you want your best interest protected. At least, you will have one less hand in your pocket.

The stock market is difficult enough without having to second-guess the motives of a stockbroker, who is paid only when you buy or sell.

YOUR RETIREMENT YEARS

Discount brokers serve a useful purpose for the serious investor who is planning for his retirement years. Learning that your investment life can make the difference in your retirement years is critical. Learning that only you care about the seriousness of this issue is vital. No stockbroker can possibly allow himself to think about your old age, as you must. The stockbroker has production schedules to meet virtually every day. You only represent a number on a computer printout. Your gross is how much you have paid in commissions to him or her. You represent leverage to your stockbroker. Brokers can negotiate a better deal for themselves, if you, and others like yourself, pay them substantial commissions.

MORE BANG FOR THE BUCK

A stockbroker tries to get "more bang for the buck" when he gets the most commissions he or she can from a given amount of money the client has. Trading options in commodities, and volatile stocks are the primary vehicles used by a stockbroker to get the most "bang for the buck."

YOU CAN'T GO BROKE TAKING A PROFIT—OR CAN YOU?

Stockbrokers typically use the phrase "You can't go broke taking a profit." Well, I disagree. If you continually sell a position just as it shows a profit, you will never make much money, and you will ultimately lose money, because you will hold one stock that goes down and down. The big money I have seen made was made over many months or years. It is very boring to many people to approach the market this way, but, are you after excitement or substantial profits and financial independence in later years? Only you can make that decision. Look carefully at yourself at night, when you are alone. You are getting older and older. If

you take care of your investments, they will take care of you. Your stockbroker will not take care of you, of that you can feel sure.

IMAGE OF KNOWLEDGE AND WISDOM

A young stockbroker said to me that he had $50,000 gross commissions in commodities during the past year. I said, "That's pretty good." "Yea," he said, "but those guys are dead; got killed in the oil market." I think this sums up the plight of the average commodity customer dealing with the average stockbroker.

JUST TRUST ME

Beware of anyone who says, "Just trust me!" Run from this fellow as fast as you can. The pressures of always meeting production schedules (commissions) distorts the concept of prudent investing for long-term goals.

You can depend on two things in good or bad times. The first is a "good dog" and the second is your "money."

A LITTLE ARSENIC

A little arsenic every day does not kill you immediately, but over a prolonged period of time, it will kill you; and be almost undetectable.

Likewise, trading in and out can kill you financially, and yet be undetectable at most any time that you look at the situation. But your capital will slowly be eaten away with commissions and taxes, if you are not very careful. Since you are buying and selling, you fail to catch the really big gains from any one situation. Typically, you will finally get into a losing situation that won't let you out, until it has really hurt you.

Basically, the only real winner in buying and selling is the stockbroker.

PROSPECTING—PORTFOLIO REVIEW

There are thousands of different combinations of techniques that a stockbroker can use to get accounts. Basically, he or she wants you to do the talking. The more you talk, the more he or she learns about you, your goals, desires, and ambitions.

Once the broker finds out that you have a portfolio (stocks, bonds, and so on), he or she will suggest that the firm run a portfolio review. I would bet that when the broker comes back with the review, you will need to sell some things and buy other things. That is what a portfolio review is good for—commissions.

Another technique the stockbroker may use is to throw the names of wealthy individuals around that he or she knows, you know, particularly if he or she comes from a wealthy family. What this has to do with doing an outstanding job for a client was always a mystery to me. I have seen absolutely awful jobs done for clients by these types. And, yet, people prefer to do business with those most familiar to them. Credentials and abilities do not seem to matter in the slightest. I would caution anyone reading these words to be very wary of individuals who want to do business with you on this basis. My experience says you are better off doing your big business with a reputable discount broker, where you can maintain an "arm's length" approach with your broker.

NEPOTISM ON WALL STREET

Stockbrokers boycott or shun those among them who truly try to help their clients with no regard for the commissions that they can get from their clients. The infrastructure of the brokerage business is very tight. Outsiders are not welcome. That is why *nepotism is so prevalent on Wall Street.* The fathers in the brokerage community hire their sons and daughters. They know of the huge amounts of money that can be made by getting their clients to buy and sell over the years. *Hundred-thousand dollar incomes are common on Wall Street* with *many million-dollar paychecks around the industry.* The leaders try to keep the huge bonuses quiet, because they do not want to "spoil a good thing" by shining the light of day on them.

Now, perhaps, you can understand why a broker who tries to be different is boycotted by the other brokers. The "nail" that stands up is going to get "hammered down" is a true saying in the brokerage business.

EQUITY HUNTERS

A young stockbroker from a wealthy family once said to me: "Don, that is why my firm and other big brokerage houses hire men like me. I know lots of people with big money. I can persuade these people to invest hundreds of thousands of dollars at a time. That is where the really big commissions are."

Note: Nothing was said about the broker's knowledge of the market, economics, and the like—just his family connections. I overheard this same young man trying to explain to a client—on the telephone—how he had lost well over $100,000 in a tax-shelter scheme. He was sweating, and his hands were shaking, because of something the irate client was saying. So you see, even the rich do not like to lose money; no matter how well they might know the family.

Once these equity hunters land a big account, they immediately try to sell them a front-end load mutual fund. Not only are the bigger commissions obtained here, but the brokers are then free to go looking for more accounts. The mutual fund manages the money, thus relieving the broker of the burden. Besides, the broker will continue to be compensated for the account, as long as the account stays with the mutual fund and the broker stays where he or she is.

MOVEMENT OF STOCKBROKERS FROM FIRM TO FIRM

I have seen entire offices of brokers move across the street to another firm. Money was the main reason. On Wall Street, money is usually the reason for everything. This type of mass movement typically occurs after a prolonged decline in the stock market. Most of the firm's clients are financially ruined, so they go to another firm and start prospecting again. They usually blame the losses on the other firm's research department. What a lot of baloney! They have just traded their clients into huge losses and need to start afresh with new clients. Of course, other stockbrokers have usually been losing also, for a major bear market takes most stocks down. Therefore, stockbrokers call on the clients of other stockbrokers, professing to know how to make the clients' money back.

It is absolutely amazing how many investors believe this rubbish year after year. Managers know that clients believe these lies. This is why they will hire a "Big Producer" or "Big Hitter" from another firm. This is a person who knows how to play the emotional heartstrings of the average investor. A "Big Producer" can generate hundreds of thousands—even millions of dollars of commissions—from his or her accounts. He or she is a "silver-tongued devil," as a friend of mine used to call these fast-talking con men.

You probably think that a broker would not stay in business, if he or she did not eventually make his or her clients money. Well, even a fool will get lucky once in a while, if he or she keeps at it long enough. A *broken clock is right twice a day without doing anything*. Most clients just take it—year after year—because they do not want to change.

Change is very difficult for most people. It requires making a decision. Most investors do not want to make decisions on their own. You would be amazed at how stockbrokers capitalize on this knowledge.

SETTLEMENT OF PURCHASES AND SALES—FIVE BUSINESS DAYS

The normal settlement period for trades is five business days. That means when you buy stock, you must *pay* the money to the brokerage firm in five business days. When you sell a stock, normally, the money from the sale can be had in five business days.

If you don't watch the brokerage firm, your payment will be delayed, if you are not adamant about payment on settlement day. I was once forced to sign an agreement form entitled Swap Check Agreement, because I wanted my money on settlement date. You might run into this situation: You sell $10,000 worth of a given stock. Four days later you decide to buy a different stock, for $8,000. You are entitled to the proceeds from your sale in five business days from the sale date. You do not owe the money for the purchase until five business days from the purchase date. However, if you don't watch it, the brokerage firm will try to pay you only the difference, and only when the purchase settles. In other words, the brokerage firm can use your credit balance for other things, while you wait for the money you are fully entitled to. Multiply this amount by millions of clients and tens of millions of dollars and you can see that the amount of money the brokerage firms stand to gain is enormous. All this is because the average investor does not know or cannot be bothered, or simply thinks the amount is insignificant. I take the attitude: "If it is important to them, it should be important to me." You should too, because if you take care of your money now, it will take care of you in the future.

I have known credit balances to lie in accounts for months with no interest paid on the money; all because the owners could not be bothered. The discount brokers I use pay you interest if you leave money in a credit balance by automatically sweeping the money into a money-market fund.

HANDSOME, SILVER-HAIRED MEN

Do not be impressed by men just because they are physically handsome, and silver-haired, and have a soft voice. *"Do not judge by appearances, but judge with right judgment,"* John 7, verse 24. I have known many such men. They can be more ruthless than you would ever believe. You must learn to make your judgments, concerning your investments, based on facts, analysis, and a great deal of common sense. When the chips are down, and you have lost all your money, these men are not going to come to your rescue. *Superficial appearances should be ignored;* look at the tangible and factual information. Ignore the hype and the "bull sh-t." Be especially careful of anyone who says: "Just trust me!" *Run, don't walk—to the nearest exit—from this type.*

TWO STOCKBROKERS TALKING IN THE COFFEE ROOM

First stockbroker: "I'll bet my stock goes back to 35."
Second stockbroker: "I'll bet my customers' losses it won't. Ha! Ha!"

THE "QUICKIE" INVESTMENT RECOMMENDATIONS

I have seen stockbrokers spend only a few minutes looking over a chart, get on the telephone, and persuade trusting investors

to put their hard-earned money into something they thought their stockbroker had given a great deal of consideration on their behalf. All the stockbrokers were looking for was a way to increase their production (commissions) for the month, so that they could get more money for their family.

I have seen trusting investors come into a brokerage office and literally spend their entire life's savings on the recommendations of some young, fast-talking broker, who pretended to be very sophisticated and professional. This same young stockbroker may have never actually invested a penny of his or her money in the marketplace. Or, even worse, the broker may be a terrible investor. There is an old adage within the brokerage industry that "a stockbroker never invests his own money for himself." No-load mutual funds and their company's stock through stock options are typical of the investments stockbrokers make for themselves. As an old stockbroker once said to me, when I asked him if he was buying what he was recommending to his clients; "Don, dear boy, this stuff is for other people's money; not for my money!" Think about it.

SEMINARS

Seminars are given by stockbrokers for sales purposes. They are nothing but sales-promotion gimmicks. They want your telephone number and your name. They use these seminars as great prospecting forums. If you think you are going to receive something for nothing, go soak your head in cold water.

These seminars are typically used to promote stockbrokers' high-commission products. Therefore, when you attend one of these "free" seminars—Beware!

COMMUNICATIONS BETWEEN MANAGERS OF DIFFERENT OFFICES

I once tried to help another investor by telling him a simple technique that would save him considerably on the commissions he would pay. Since I knew the brokerage firm's system of giving discounts on the sell side, I thought I would help him. This is always a mistake! "Keep your mouth shut," is the best advice I can ever give you.

The investor I tried to help went straight to the manager and demanded the same discount I was getting on the east coast. He was furious because a total stranger and a man twenty years his junior from another part of the country had told him something his own stockbroker had not told him; after all those years of paying full commissions.

A few days later *my* discount was rescinded. In other words the manager at the office where I tried to help a fellow investor called the manager at the office on the east coast, where my main account was held, and had my discount voided. So much for helping other investors.

The "lesson" you should learn is *"Keep your damn mouth shut when you get a better deal than someone else."* Also, *do not trust stockbrokers or managers of brokerage offices. They are not your friend.* They are taking care of their retirement and their family. Always remember this fact, as long as you live. Once you are old and worn out, you will find out that I am telling you the truth. It will be too late, then.

A *manager of a member firm, and a vice-president, said to me one morning over coffee: "You know, Don, stockbrokers are like WHORES! They will—anybody for a commission."* These are not my words, but the words of a successful manager. It is not the first time I have heard it said, either.

CHINESE WALL

The separation between the investment banking side of a member firm and the brokerage side of a member firm is called the Chinese Wall. It is invisible, but it is supposed to exist. The investment banking is where the member firm deals with their corporate clients. The brokerage side is where the member firm deals with the public at large. The *public business* is referred to, within the industry, as the *retail trade,* or the *peanut gallery.*

TESTS TAKEN BY STOCKBROKERS

Copies of similar or exact questions on the stockbrokers' exams are supplied by prompters weeks before the exams. The questions are worked and reworked. There is very little, if anything, that is left to chance. This is not knowledge, this is memory work, and it has nothing to do with making money in the marketplace. Stockbrokers are hired to open accounts and sell the companies' products—to generate commissions.

There are schools set up around the country specifically for training salespeople to take these tests—and pass! I have attended several of these classes for different exams. When these people have finished going over their material, the student knows the test—almost by heart.

SALES ASSISTANTS

Sales assistants, who are usually young women, give quotes on stock prices and act friendly. Remember their titles: sales assistants. They are there to assist the broker. They can very subtly say things on the telephone that will prompt you to take action, when you had no intention of taking any such action when you called. Remember, *the mission of the brokerage office is to generate sales for the firm—not profits for you.*

FINANCIAL NEWS ANNOUNCERS

It never ceases to amaze me how confident financial news announcers can appear to be. However, when you record what they say in your diary, you will find out, over the years, just how awful their forecasting really is. And, yet, they will come on the television again and again and continue to spew out their garbage with the same apparent self-confidence. There should be some accountability forced on these phonies. If they were exposed, for what they really know, the investing public would be at least tens of millions of dollars ahead.

These reporters are famous for using extremes in reporting the market; e.g., the market "plunged" today; the market "soared" today; the "bulls" ran "rampant" on Wall Street today; the "debacle" in the dollar took traders by surprise; "panic" hit Wall Street today.

Then, of course, there are the "blacks": "Black" Monday, "Black" Tuesday, "Black" Wednesday, and so on.

Why do so many investors expect something for nothing? Why do investors think these types are going to give them advice that is going to stuff money into their pockets—for nothing? I have heard it said that "the greatest desert in the world is in the head of the average investor." Think about it!

PROVERBS 24, VERSES 3,4,5

By wisdom a house is built, and by understanding it is established; by knowledge the rooms are filled with all precious and pleasant riches. A wise man is mightier than a strong man, and a man of knowledge than he who has strength.

PROVERBS 23, VERSE 9

Do not speak in the hearing of a fool, for he will despise the wisdom of your words.

DISCOUNT BROKERS

Doing business with a discount broker is a refreshing experience. No hard sell; no pushing of products; no intimidation. Just fast executions at very low commissions. I have found that the information you get about your account, news items on your stocks, tender-offer information, and most anything factual is better at a reputable discount broker.

THE REALLY SMART STOCKBROKERS

Within the inner workings of the major brokerage firms, there are extremely smart and savvy individuals. These people really do know a great deal about what has happened, is happening, and what will probably happen. Most of you will never know or do business with these people. These individuals are not like the stockbrokers sitting on the front line of your local brokerage office. The local stockbroker is a salesperson—pure and simple.

These upper-echelon people are the "movers and shakers" in the real world of finance. A million dollars per year—and up—is standard pay; not a big deal at all for these individuals. Unfortunately, most of you think you are getting the same information they are getting—at the same time. Please do not think that ever again. Use your common sense and you will realize you, the retail client, in Main Street, USA, are at the end of the line, not the beginning.

You must realize the stockbrokers are going to stuff money into their pockets long before they put money into your pockets.

HOW ABUSING OF ACCOUNTS IS BLAMED ON THE STOCKBROKER

Have you ever noticed when a stockbroker is found guilty of a securities crime, he has usually resigned months earlier? But the manager is usually still there.

Although the manager is constantly pushing the retail brokers to produce more and more, the head of the broker is served up as a sacrifice, when the house of cards comes falling down. This is much like the military. Rarely will you find the head of an important general falling. A captain, major, or even a colonel will fall long before a general. Usually, an *enlisted man* will be made the scapegoat—or a young lieutenant.

So it is with the brokerage business. The troops in the trenches are expendable, whereas the leaders continue operating as though nothing has happened.

PROFESSIONAL MANAGEMENT

Professional management is a way of putting the burden of performance on someone else, while the stockbroker gets a piece

of the action (commissions). The client's money is handled by some stranger who charges a management fee. You would be surprised how many ways there are to carve up your money in management fees, redemption fees, and commissions. And, yet, investors continue to pay dearly when they could spend a little time on weekends and learn for themselves. The enormous amount of money they could save is unbelievable; but most of you will not do it.

BEWARE OF PATRONIZING VOICES

Beware of patronizing voices that tell you, "You don't want to do thus and so; I know what is best for you!" There are very few individuals who really know what is best for you.

When a stockbroker or investment adviser becomes indignant because you question his or her advice or ideas, let him or her know—in no uncertain terms—that *it is your money,* not his or her money, that is being *invested and risked.* It is your decision, in the final analysis, and if you lose, the losses will be your losses. Therefore, speak up and defend your best interest—no one else will!

A *mistake I made when dealing with stockbrokers* in my naive days was: *I tried to fight clean. Forget it!* They have only one main thing on their minds: *commissions.* The sooner you get that through your head, the better off you will be. You will never change Wall Street. *Learn to be hard and demanding.* To be forewarned is to be forearmed!

INVESTORS OF ALL TYPES

I have seen college professors, doctors of all types, lawyers, and most any professional group you can name participate in the stock market. Most of them think their stockbroker is their friend and has their best interest at heart. *Investors are wrong on both counts, usually.*

Stockbrokers must sell their company's products for a commission or leave the business. You may think this is obvious. However, until you have had your account churned, you cannot possibly know how it feels; or the damage that can happen so quickly to your money.

It does not matter how many commissions you paid a broker last year. The only thing that counts is, What are you going to do for him or her today? The past is a cancelled check. The future is a promissory note. Only today counts on a production (commission) printout. All the good intentions in the world count for nothing in the securities business.

The managers are paid to keep the pressure on their stockbrokers for more and more commissions. If you get hurt in the process, then you only have yourself to blame.

LESSON: Get this parasite off your back or he will "break" you.

DEK

You must learn to say no. You must learn to use a reputable discount broker. You must *learn to think for yourself.*

POLITICS WITHIN A BROKERAGE OFFICE

Politics is vicious within the typical brokerage office, where stockbrokers compete to see who sells the most of a secondary offering, primary offering, or other issues in which the firm has a piece of the action. There is very little regard for the clients' making money, as long as the firm has a favorable recommen-

dation on the issue. This assures the stockbroker that the firm's entire legal staff is behind him or her, if the issue blows up in the investor's faces.

FRONT-END MONEY

Front-end money, or very high payouts of up to 100 percent of the first few month's commissions are two of many techniques used to lure big producers (stockbrokers who can generate lots of commissions from their clients' accounts) away from their present employer. Little do the clients know how much leverage their broker has, because of the client's trust in the stockbroker. For that trust, the clients are encouraged to buy and sell excessively and often only in the stockbroker's best interest. Whether the clients make money or not is incidental to the entire transaction.

Commissions are the name of the game. If the client loses, well, they have a tax loss. Either way, the stockbroker makes out. And all of this is *perfectly legal—SO LONG AS THE INVESTOR APPROVES EVERY TRADE; IF NOT, THEN THE CLIENT HAS GROUNDS FOR LEGAL ACTION!*

A LICENSE TO STEAL

Many years ago a car salesman became a stockbroker with the firm I was with. The car salesman turned to me one evening, after work, and said: "Man, you guys have a license to steal in this business. I am going to have a ball."

BANNED FROM ENTERING THE BROKER'S OFFICE

When you enter a brokerage office, it is at the invitation of the firm, whether you know it or not. It is private property. You can be banned or barred from entering the office under penalty of arrest. I have seen this happen. No matter how much you have spent in commissions and interest charges, you can literally be prevented from coming back into the office. I thought you should know, in the event you thought you were buying goodwill with all those dollars you have spent at your local brokerage office.

FEAR

As one manager of a local brokerage office said: "We are dealing with *fear*—fear that the stockbroker will be fired, if he does not meet the commission schedule the firm has established. In fact, the *fear* is so great the young brokers spend so much time trying to figure out how to do the required 135,000 in gross commissions for their first year, they do not have time to plan on how to do 175,000 or more in commissions."

CLOAK OF SECRECY

Stockbrokers place a big cloak of secrecy on what they do. They lead many of their clients to think they are really doing them a favor when they give them a small discount. The manager of a major member firm whispered to me: "Do not tell anybody about this *discount!" I wanted to "puke!"* Why? because *the lie was so obvious.* I was getting a bigger discount in several other places; bigger than the discount he was giving me under such a cloak of secrecy. Even with the same firm, I was getting the same discount at another branch, and I was getting a better overall discount at still another branch of the same firm; both branches were in different states other than the state in question.

He tried so hard to make me think that he had really gone to bat for me. What a joke! *Managers are not your friend, they are company men—through and through!* And bear in mind that many of them make hundreds of thousands of dollars, and more, every year. So what do you think is more important to them—your little account or their fat paycheck and pension?

These people are also not above lying to you. Not only have I caught them in lie after lie, but when I would confront them, they would say something like: "So what," or "Big deal!"

When these individuals promise you that "It is in the mail," make sure you receive the material before you do anything. Many times I have been told "It is in the mail," when, in fact, it was not. When I followed up on it, and asked where it was, one stockbroker smiled and said, "Don, you know I can't really mail that to you. It is against company policy." When I asked why he lied to me, he said, *"Don, most people do not want the truth. Lying is better."*

WHY INVESTORS TRUST STOCKBRROKERS

" . . . they are so forgiving." Investors, that is. "Because they think other people (stockbrokers) know more about it than themselves, so they feel intimidated."

FJK—My daughter, July 29, 1987

BOARDROOM SITTERS

Most people who spend time in brokerage office boardrooms are retired. They may dabble in the market, but very few of them have serious money committed to stocks as a speculation. Only after interviewing many elderly men in many boardrooms (brokerage offices), did I find out that they are there to "kill" time; not make a "killing" in the market.

I was shocked to find that most of them had never read any serious books on the stock market. I thought they were as serious as I was. I thought they were as committed to the stock market as I was. Not true. Repeatedly, I was told, "Don, I need a place to come to, to get out of the house. I have my retirement; I have it made. I don't need to take any chances."

THE METAMORPHOSIS OF A COMMODITY BROKER TURNED MANAGER

When I saw a broker, who had been a big commodity broker-producer, give his commodity books away to a new, younger broker, I knew something was up. The older broker had received a promotion. He was through just trading commodities for a more predictable and less hectic job with the same firm. I have seen this happen more than once.

What about all his customers who had paid enormous commissions to him over the years? They actually thought he cared about their future. All he was interested in was furthering his career. What about the families of those customers who lost so much buying and selling and losing? "Sorry about that," is a common phrase used in the business; or "that's life," as one broker said to me.

What about the architect who had to sell his beautiful home, uproot his family, and leave town? All this happened because he lost everything in the silver market. When I asked him how it had happened, he said, "I listened to the razzle-dazzle of my stockbroker. He literally hypnotized me with his smooth talk. And, of course, it was so exciting. I really thought I was going to make a fortune." I asked him if he blamed the stockbroker. "Only to the extent that I would never have known about the fast game of commodities, had it not been for my broker," he said. *"I really did not know that commodity traders could be so vicious!"*

STOP ORDERS

In my twenty years of speculating, investing, and watching hundreds of others do the same, I can tell you one thing about stop orders: *They are great for generating commissions for stockbrokers. They are great for getting you out on sharp sell-offs. However, you are not assured of your price on a straight stop.* I have seen "gaps" where the stop was executed many points away from the stop price. That is because the *stop order becomes a market order* once the stop price or a lower price is triggered—on a sell-stop, of course. A buy-stop order would work on the up side of a stock exactly the opposite to a sell-stop order.

I have never personally known one serious investor who made a lot of money who used mechanical stop orders. I have seen successful men set predetermined points in their mind at which they would buy or sell, but not mechanical devices. The other point is that when such a point is set in your mind, it should be used on a long-term basis. In other words, you should not get out and jump right back in; otherwise, why get nervous at that predetermined level in the first place? The market can whipsaw you to death, if you try this very often.

OPTIONS—WASTING ASSETS

Stockbrokers love for you to trade options because of several reasons:

1. You have to pay cash immediately for them, thus no risk to the firm's capital.
2. You tend to turn over the money quicker; ergo, more and more commissions.
3. More excitement; more conversation leading to other activities.

Options are a great vehicle for generating commissions for the brokerage community. They are also useful for sophisticated investors who truly understand hedging and risk management. Unfortunately, many average investors think they are sophisticated, or they think their broker is. Only after huge losses occur will most investors realize the true complexities of option trading.

Since I have seen a great deal of financial bloodshed in the options markets, my advice to most of you is: Don't waste your time and money trading options. Look toward undervalued securities that you can pay for and have them delivered out to you. Put them in your safety-deposit box. Let time be your friend; not your enemy.

DEATH WISH OF A CLIENT

If clients allow their account to be *churned by their stockbrokers,* then they have a *death wish.* The stockbroker is going to get commissions from the accounts for as long as possible. When one gets accustomed to a free lunch, one is not going to give it up willingly, or voluntarily. I would not have set out on this journey to write a book, had I not become so disgusted with what I have seen as a stockbroker, myself, or as a client.

As long as a client knows that the commissions are the paramount consideration of the stockbroker, then the client is, at least, armed with the truth. I feel sure that many stockbrokers will be up in arms to protest this book. But let them deny the truth of its contents to the faces of their clients!

IF YOU REFUSE TO THINK FOR YOURSELF

If you refuse to think for yourself and depend on your stockbroker, you are placing your trust in an individual with a direct conflict of interest. Would you place a *fox in charge of your "henhouse?"*

BUST THAT ORDER

If a stockbroker does not submit your order exactly as you instructed, you have the right to order the stockbroker to "bust"

the trade. The broker will not like it, especially if there is a loss on the trade, but you have the right. A stockbroker has no right to alter your order in any way. That is why it is called an order. Remember, it is your money; do not allow anyone to be careless with it.

FINANCIAL ADVISORY LETTERS

I could tell you about the dozens of investment information services I have taken from time to time; but the salient points will be made without mentioning the individual services. To tell you the truth, I never really did very well as a result of the advice of these services. I found they were useful as sales tools when I was a stockbroker. My clients, as well as other stockbrokers, and their clients were impressed that I had so much information. However, the goal of an investor should be to make large gains—and keep them. This leads me to the points about services that I have found to be true as a group. I recognize there are exceptions to everything, but the following is what I have found as a rule.

Each service is pushing a particular idea or philosophy. They may recommend using charts, fundamentals, or both. The services may be eternal optimists or pessimists. Some may say gold is the only answer, but suggest trading stocks with sophisticated techniques. There are so many services trying so many things with other people's money that I could not begin to cover them all. Therefore, the important thing for you to remember is this: *You are after investments that you can live with, depending upon your temperament, and keeping in mind your investment objectives. You can spend a little time looking through the material I am going to present to you and, I believe, do just as well as, or better than, these services who want your money—year after year.*

If they knew so much, they could be billionaires in short order, just investing their money. They make so many recommendations over the months and years that they must hit a winner from time to time. But how do you know which one will go up and which will stay the same, or go down? These letter writers state their case so convincingly that the average investor assumes they must be right in their analysis. Otherwise, they wouldn't be allowed to keep writing such things. Right? Wrong! Wrong! Wrong!

Since knowledge is power, I urge you to study and read books that try to teach you to look at the bigger picture. Economics can be interesting, challenging, and very rewarding. *Think for yourself!*

SOPHISTICATED—AND STUPID

Too many people think they are being sophisticated when they get into the stock market—especially during the heat of battle, when volume is high and the majority of stocks are making highs, with very few lows in sight. Unfortunately, I have seen more losses come from environments like this than any other time. Once the market starts down, no one rings a bell to say the music has stopped. Human nature being what it is, most individuals wait for just one more rally, to get out with a profit.

Down at the lows, after many margin accounts have been liquidated, voluntarily or involuntarily, by the brokerage firms, very few individuals have the courage to buy when the true values are available. They still remember their losses of recent times.

In other words, when they really should be buying, they are selling—and scared to death.

CONFESSIONS OF SOME STOCKBROKERS

I have had stockbrokers confide in me that, "yes, the way brokers are paid contributes to a conflict of interest." However, they have to make a living and they are not going to change Wall Street. Until the average investor "wises up," things will remain as they are. Discount brokers are changing Wall Street very slowly.

Chapter 2

The Most Important Cycles—for Most Investors—that Repeat Consistently

PATTERNS THAT TEND TO REPEAT

Cycles: The Science of Prediction was written by Edward R. Dewey and Edwin F. Dakin. It was published by Henry Holt and Co. in 1947. This is one of the most important books on cycles ever published in my opinion.

A number of patterns tend to repeat on a consistent basis over the years in the financial world. The following chapter covers some of the repetitive patterns that will assist you the most in your study of the stock and bond markets.

FORTY-MONTH CYCLE

Of the many cycles discussed in the *Cycles,* the forty-month or three and one half-year cycle has helped me so much on so many occasions that I bring it to your attention. The Foundation for the Study of Cycles was kind enough to give me permission to reprint Gertrude Shirk's interpretation of how the cycle looks graphically.

You will notice that the rise is rather consistent until near the top, where it tends to accelerate and then falls off sharply on the back side of the curve or graph. Stocks also tend to behave in this manner. This is one of the reasons for the old Wall Street saying that the market rises three-quarters of the time and falls one quarter of the time, but the fall is much faster than the rise.

The 40-Month Cycle in Stock Prices*

The riddle of the length of the 38- to 52-month cycle in stock prices has not, in my opinion, been solved in a satisfactory manner. A lot of work has been done on the problem and one fact which has emerged from this work might be of some interest.

"Stock prices" in this case refers to the monthly record of average prices which starts in 1789 and which uses the Dow-Jones Industrials for the current figures. These data have been filtered to remove trend, to enhance any 40-month cycle, and to depress any longer and shorter cycles. When these filtered data are summarized, it develops that, despite the recent ambiguity of the cycle, the time spent in going up or going down averages about 19 to 20 months.

(The following graph) illustrates this point. Over the history of the 57 repetitions of the cycle as revealed by the filtered data, a total of 114 moves up and down have occurred. When these are tabulated according to the number of months that each move covers, the most common span of time has been 20 months. The shortest span was 9 months; this length occurred three times. The longest move was 29 months; this length occurred once.

The average length was 19.07 months, the median length was 19.03 months, and the mode was 20.4 months.

POLITICAL-BUSINESS CYCLE

Fortune magazine had an excellent article entitled "Riding the Political-Business Cycle" in its September 22, 1980, issue by Robert Lubar. In the article Mr. Lubar points out that "Within an incumbent's term of office there is a predictable pattern of policy, starting with relative austerity in early years and ending with the potlatch right before elections."

Said another way, *the incumbent president will tighten the screws down through rising interest rates and rising unemployment in the first two years or so of his administration. In this way much of the inflation*

*Reprinted by permission from "The 40-Month Cycle in Stock Prices," by Gertrude Shirk, *Cycles,* November 1982 (Pittsburgh: Foundation for the Study of Cycles).

The 40-Month Cycle in Stock Prices

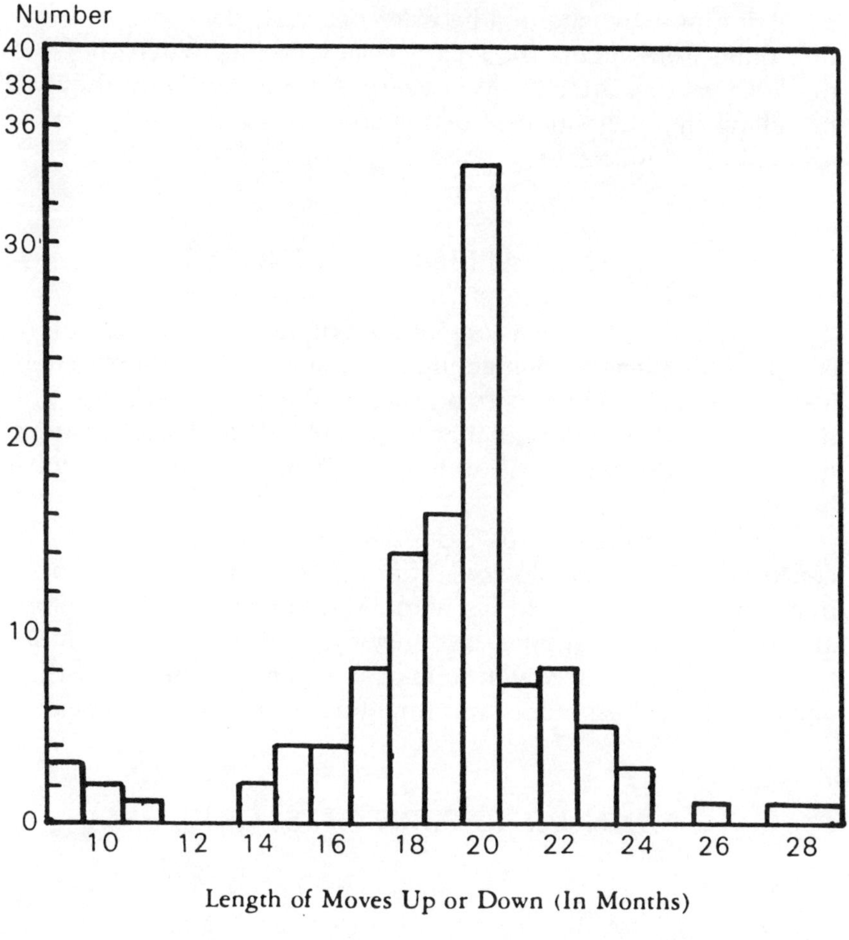

Dow-Jones Industrials—Data Filtered for 40-Month Cycles:
Number of Moves by Length of Moves

caused by the last two years of the previous administration can be squeezed out. This allows him the same privilege—inflating in the last two years of his administration so the voters will vote for him, or his party's nominee in the next election.

A word of caution: The presidential election year can be very deceiving and treacherous because many stocks top out during this time. Remember, the smart money bought when the stock market was low after the two years of austerity. Now they will be selling in anticipation of two years of austerity after the presidential election, again.

THE FALLING DOMINOS

Morgan Maxfield was one of the brightest young men I have ever had the pleasure of meeting in the late 1970s. Unfortunately, Morgan was killed in an airplane accident in the early 1980s. Still, he left behind some original and valuable ideas. I was fortunate to have asked his permission to quote from his writings prior to his death.

The "Falling Dominos"* depicts, pictorially, Morgan's ideas concerning the chronological order of events that tend to occur in a repetitive pattern. In his work, Morgan changed these items around from time to time, but enclosed is the one I have found the most useful. I urge you to take some of your time and think about each of these items and how this cycle tends to repeat.

ANNUAL RETURN ON STOCKS

David Dreman, in his book *Contrarian Investment Strategy: The Psychology of Stock Market Success,* has done an outstanding service for all of us. In the illustration on page 83, he indicates how the return on common stocks can fluctuate from year to year.** How-

*Reprinted by permission from *Economic Meteorology* by Morgan Maxfield.

**Reprinted by permission of the publisher from *Contrarian Investment Strategy: The Psychology of Stock Market Success* by David Dreman (New York: Random House, Inc., 1979).

THE FALLING DOMINOS

ever, if you look carefully, you will notice some very important patterns. Take a year that you know was down sharply, then look at the following year's performance. Likewise, take a year that you know was up sharply, then observe the following year's performance. These patterns are very important to you. Take the time to think about them. Get a chart book of long-term graphs of stocks, bonds, and the indexes over fifty years or so. You will begin to notice that these patterns tend to repeat—over and over.

BONDS AND INTEREST RATES

The bond market traditionally leads the stock market up and down. Why? Maybe the more sophisticated investor is involved with the bond market. Once the Federal Reserve tightens money, short-term rates move up. Then, the long-term rates move up, if it is perceived that the tightening is of a longer-term significance. Then, *the stock market will eventually begin to weaken because the stock market does not like rising interest rates.*

Sear that information into your brain forever. High interest rates have killed almost all of the big bull markets in history. Many analysts will cite this or that reason for the last big bear market. But remember that high interest rates will kill a stock market quicker than anything I know. As interest rates rise, long-term, the bond prices will fall to adjust to the new interest-rate level. Of course, if interest rates fall, bond prices will rise because the bonds have fixed coupons.

A bond with a fixed coupon can only be competitive with other bonds through price. Therefore, as interest rates rise, bond prices fall; as interest rates fall, bond prices rise.

When interest rates reach historic levels on long-term bonds, investors should place more and more of their capital in these rich yields. Unfortunately, many investors are scared to death and stay in short-term money-market funds or short-term certificates of deposit.

Many investors fail to realize that huge gains can be made in the bond market when interest rates are declining; pushing bond prices up sharply.

Annual return on stocks, 1926–1978.

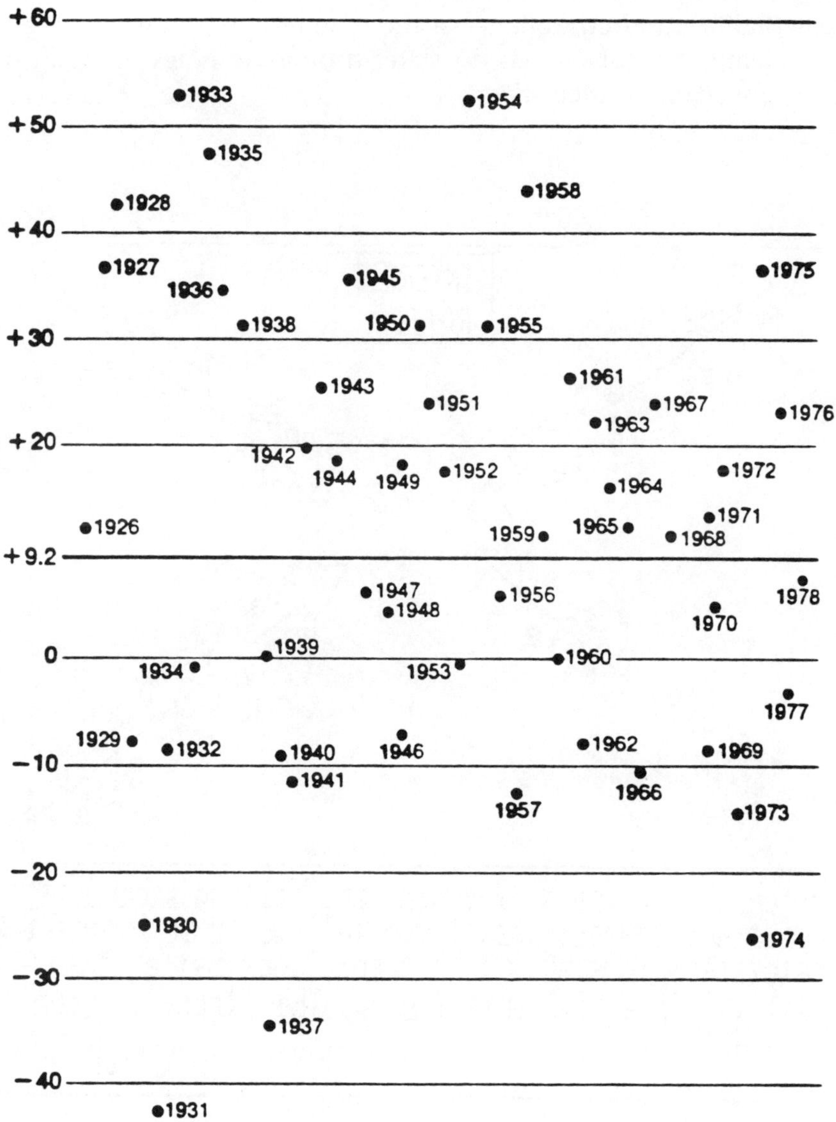

U.S. goverment T-bills, notes, and bonds can be purchased in almost unlimited amounts for a commission charge of forty or fifty dollars. In other words, no matter how many you buy, the commission charge at many reputable discount brokers would be less than a hundred dollars—at the time of this writing.

Remember, also, that no state income tax is levied against U.S. government securities.

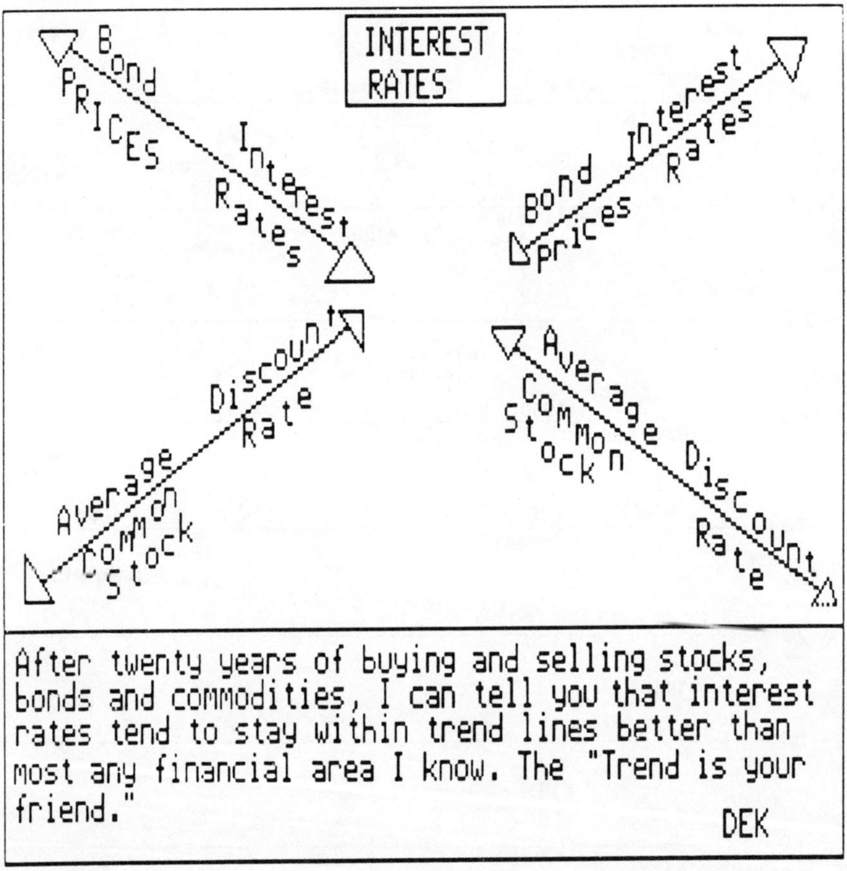

After twenty years of buying and selling stocks, bonds and commodities, I can tell you that interest rates tend to stay within trend lines better than most any financial area I know. The "Trend is your friend."

DEK

STOCK PRICE DECLINES AND MONETARY CONDITIONS

The following graph depicts the relationship between the length of monetary ease and stock prices.* I found this on page 467 of James Dines's book, *How the Average Investor Can Use Technical Analysis for Stock Profits.* You will reap many financial rewards in your financial lifetime if you take the time to really appreciate this information.

STOCK PRICE DECLINES AND MONETARY CONDITIONS

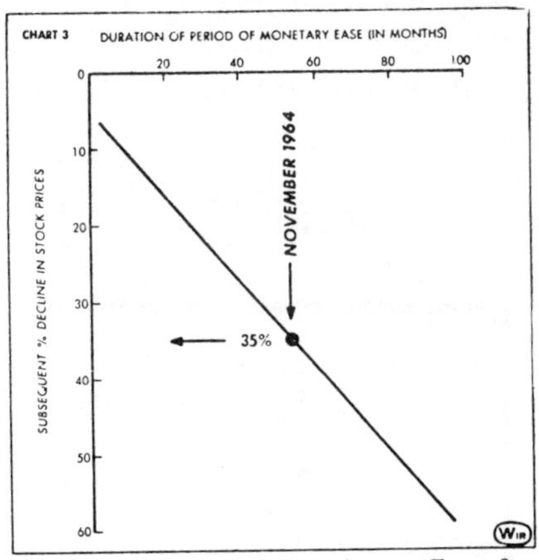

History shows a tendency for stock price declines to vary in severity with the duration of the preceding period of easy money. The relationship is shown graphically in the chart at the right. The duration of the period of monetary ease in months is shown by the scale at the top of the chart; the corresponding subsequent percentage decline in stock prices is shown by the vertical scale at the left of the chart.

As shown by Chart 2 on page 3 we are currently in the ninth period of tightening money and credit. These are shown by the shaded portions of the chart. The unshaded portions are periods of easing monetary conditions.

The relationship of stock price declines to the duration of preceding periods of easy money was calculated by arranging in descending order the two sets of figures. The figures were then smoothed by moving averages and a 'least squares fit' calculated. This is the slanted line shown on Chart 3.

November 1964, when the period of easy money (according to our definition) ended with the third rise in the Moni-Vane, was the 53rd month of easy money conditions. Based upon past relationships, 53 months of easy money would suggest a subsequent stock price decline of approximately 35%.

This relationship of stock prices to monetary conditions is only approximate, of course but it does serve to suggest the degree of risk to stock prices implicit in developing monetary conditions.

*Reprinted by permission from *How the Average Investor Can Use Technical Analysis for Stock Profits,* James Dines & Co., P.O. Box 22, Belvedere, Ca. 94920. Underlining added by the author.

P/E RATIO CYCLE

$$\frac{\text{PRICE OF THE STOCK}}{\text{EARNINGS PER SHARE}} = \text{P/E RATIO}$$

P/E ratios can be very misleading to the average investor. A P/E ratio reflects the earnings of last year relative to the present stock price. Most amateurs look at the P/E ratio without really understanding what it means. Professionals look at the future prospects and try to project future earnings, not past earnings.

In February 1981, a leading market expert said he would not buy the auto stocks because they were losing money. I remember when he was so very bullish on Ford in the 40s in 1978 and 1979. However, in 1981, with the stock under 20, he said on television that he would not buy Ford because it was losing money.

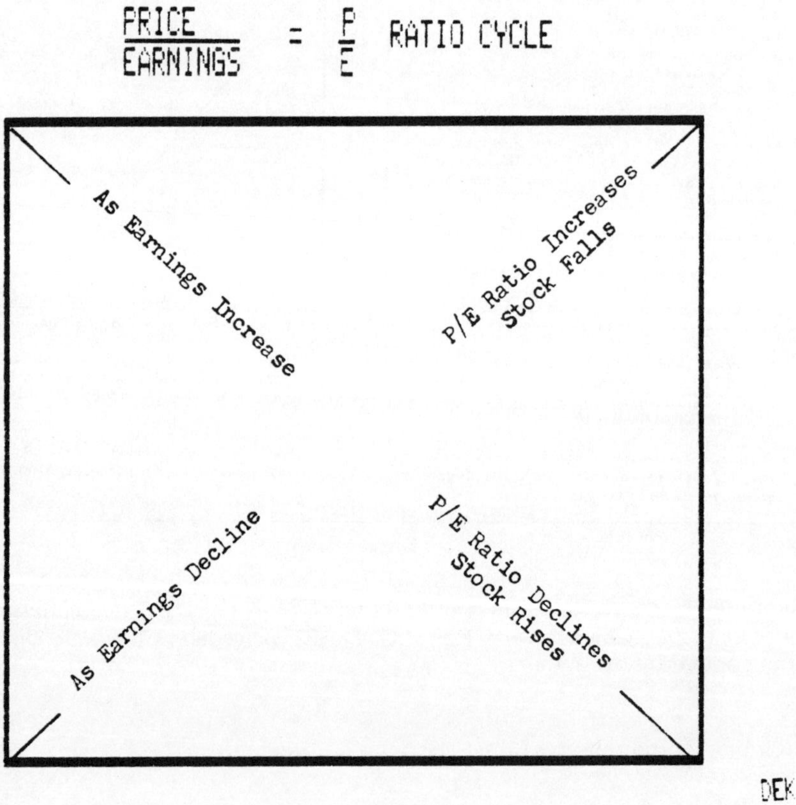

Ironically, Ford and Chrysler were making important, long-term lows around this time. In other words, when these stocks were truly a value (undervalued), there were few analysts who were openly optimistic. There were buyers, of course, but who were they? Who, we don't know; but smart, we do know! That is why it is so important to remember: the *best values are found in pessimism: the best sales are found in optimism.*

P/E ratios were at infinity at the lows because there were no earnings; this is when they were truly undervalued—and sold out. This is the time when the smart investors quietly buy. You must buy straw hats in the winter so that you can buy low; then sell the same straw hats in the summer when they are in demand. So it is with stocks.

At a major top in these stocks, the P/E ratios will be 2 or 3 or 4 or some very low number because the earnings will be great. This is the time that the smart investors will very quietly sell.

THE TYPICAL INVESTOR'S CYCLE

I found the following graph in James Dines' book: *How The Average Investor Can Use Technical Analysis For Stock Profits.** This is one variation describing the emotions of the typical investor. Mr. Dines labeled it: A Typical Small Investor's Cycle. However, I have found it to be typical of many large investors also.

I find it amazing that it is so accurate in its description of the average investor's behavior. Take some time to think about this graph. The time horizon is not labeled, but I have found this is typical of the forty-month cycle, although other time horizons could apply to specific stocks, industries or commodities.

*Reprinted by permission from *How the Average Investor Can Use Technical Analysis for Stock Profits,* James Dines & Co., P.O. Box 22, Belvedere, Ca. 94920

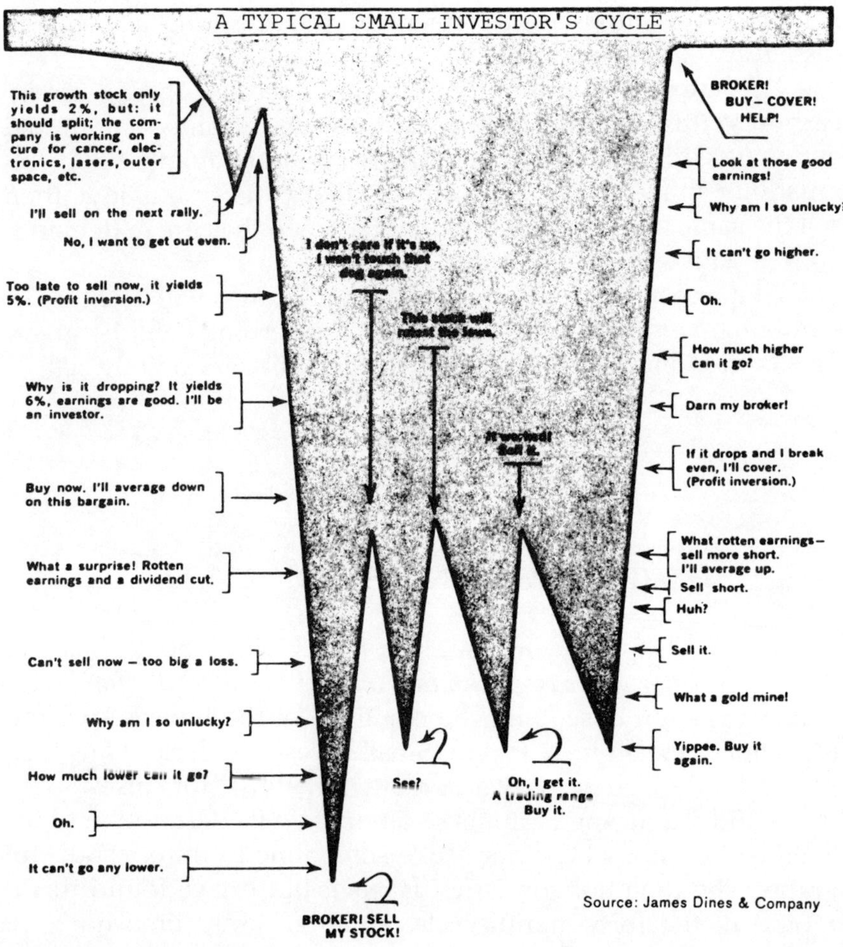

Source: James Dines & Company

THE BIG PICTURE

I break every year into twelve parts for each month of the year. Each month is broken down into two parts: the buys and the sells. I use a poster board twenty-two inches by twenty-eight inches. It is usually placed in a private location so no one but myself can see it. However, it could be placed anywhere.

The important point is for you to be able to see clearly what you are doing. This idea has helped me see where my buying and selling has tended to occur the most. This is an excellent method of stopping you from being emotional about your decisions. Try using this idea for a few years and you will see how helpful it can be. Be sure and keep the poster boards for future reference.

If you forget October in March, you will regret it in December.

Buys: J	Buys: F	Buys: M	Buys: A	Buys: M	Buys: J
Sells:	Sells:	Sells:	Sells:	Sells:	Sells:
Buys: J	Buys: A	Buys: S	Buys: O	Buys: N	Buys: D
Sells	Sells:	Sells:	Sells:	Sells:	Sells:

Chapter 3

Investment Techniques and Ideas that Can Work Consistently—for You. Secrets of the Trade!

DOCUMENT EVERYTHING IN YOUR DIARY

Buy yourself a large diary, an 8.5 by 14 inch is a very good size. Document all telephone calls. Keep all recommendations by stockbrokers, insurance salespeople, and mutual fund salespeople in your diary. Get everything that they recommend to you in writing on their company's letterhead. Insist on it. If they do not want to put it in writing on their company's letterhead—hang up! Figure you are money ahead because you probably will be. Honest men have nothing to hide and will put their recommendations in writing.

Free information is usually worth just what you pay for it . . . nothing! Why would anyone give you free, valuable information so you can make money on it? If it was that good, they would keep it all to themselves, wouldn't they? Use time as your ally. If you have to take action immediately, pass it up. I have seen a lot of good deals come and go. Almost all the really good ideas gave me plenty of time to think about them and make sensible and prudent decisions. "Haste makes waste" is surely true in the investment arena. Learn to be cynical.

A BROAD LIST OF IDEAS TO CONSIDER

Always have a long-term chart of the issue under consideration in front of you. Some excellent chart services with long-term graphs are: Securities Research, Value Line, and Moody's.

1. Buy when stock prices are low, out of favor, and undervalued. (Low is not necessarily undervalued.)
2. Make your investments based on long-term cycles. Ignore the short-term, day-to-day fluctuations.
3. Look for an investment theme within the market.
4. Look for large holdings by officers of the firm.
5. Do not follow stockbrokers' advice blindly.
6. Investigate for yourself. See with your own eyes.
7. Establish selling targets for part of your position when you buy.
8. *Be aware of percentage moves, not absolute dollar moves.*
9. Develop discipline in your dealings with stockbrokers.
10. Be firm. Ask for no favors, give no latitude in your account, *NO DISCRETIONARY ORDERS!* Take a day or a week to review any suggestions. If you are asked to act quickly, pass it up. Yes, you may miss an opportunity or two, but you will also miss out on a lot of losses.
11. Do not try to run before you can walk. You may get lucky; however, I doubt it will happen very often. The road to riches on Wall Street is rarely paved with luck. You must develop discipline, knowledge, wisdom, and patience. You must learn where your stress points are, as Roy W. Longstreet pointed out in his book, *Viewpoints of a Commodity Trader.* Do not let your greed override your common sense. There are always opportunities if you have capital, knowledge, and time.

The average investors seem to be afraid of stocks when they are real bargains. They will buy with wild enthusiasm at the next top; when they should be selling. What they were too afraid to buy at the low points, they gladly buy after 100 percent, 200 percent, and more increases. Most investors I have known over the last twenty years spent too much time trying to keep up with the Joneses and what they were buying and selling! Rarely, have I found innovative ideas from the average investor. Most investors seem to spend their time listening to other people's ideas. They try to emulate or copy the winners. This is very often a serious mistake. Think for yourself.

THE BEST LEADING ECONOMIC INDICATOR

Stock prices tend to lead the U.S. economy. The stock prices are often a more reliable indicator than any other. The reason, I suspect, is that the really smart people vote with their money, what they believe. "Talk is cheap," but their action is a more reliable indicator, especially their money actions.

NEGOTIABLE ITEMS ON YOUR INVESTMENTS

Commissions: Virtually every item is negotiable. Commission charges on stocks, bonds, commodities—the whole ball of wax—are negotiable. An excellent guide is to check several reputable discount brokers. See what they are charging. I have even negotiated a discount from a very large discount broker. The larger your account, the more bargaining power you have. Money talks—on Wall Street—so speak up!

Interest Rates on Margin Accounts: Interest rates are very negotiable on margin accounts at most major brokerage offices. Use the broker-loan rate as a guide for your negotiations. Some large discount brokers let you borrow *at broker-loan rates.* They figure they will make their money on the commissions you will pay buying and selling the marginable positions. And there are other, less obvious advantages to the firm. In other words, margin accounts are very profitable for brokerage firms.

BUY ON 50 PERCENT RETRACEMENT

Buy a stock on a 50 percent retracement from an all-time high of the previous move. For instance, a stock moves from 20 to 40, and 40 was a new high. Then, it pulls back. 100 percent of the move would be 20 points; therefore, 50% retracement would be 10 points. At 30, you should consider buying. You will be amazed how many stocks move up to unbelievable heights by moving in this manner.

SECRETS OF THE TRADE IN ANALYZING MARKETS

Actually, the following are not secrets, so much as the average investor does not want to recognize the simple way they work. Investors seem to look for complicated and confusing answers that do not work for very long.

Identifying major trends is much more important than daily fluctuations. The following should help you enormously—if you have patience, money, and the willingness to see a position through to the finish:

1. $\frac{\text{Dow-Jones Industrial Average}}{\text{Annual Dividend of the DJIA}}$

   When this ratio is 30+, market is high.
   When under 15, market is low.

2. 10Q and 10K reports on the company. These are the reports that are filed with the Securities and Exchange Commissions. This information is much more detailed than the quarterly and annual reports sent to stockholders. The company will send you a free copy—if you write and ask for a copy.

3. Benjamin Graham had a number of ideas that are excellent. However, it is very difficult to explain why so many excellent companies that do so well do not fall into his buy areas. Therefore, I would say the following:
   a. Avoid companies with huge debt structures in cyclical industries. Even if they go up from time to time, I think these stocks are better left alone.
   b. Cash: Look for companies with clean balance sheets, i.e., little or no debt, a current ratio of three to one or higher. Very little dilution of equity through convertible bonds, convertible preferred stock, warrants, or other devices is important.

4. A leader in its field.

5. Stock buy-back program by the company. If institutions or

large investors have committed large amounts of money to the stock, you should look at it. Study 13D filings in *Barron's* every week.

6. Look for an entire industry that has been depressed for some time, but the fundamentals seem likely to improve. If you see the entire industry begin to come to life, this is usually a good buy signal.

7. If interest rates have been high for quite some time, and the stock market has been depressed, this is usually a good indication that the trend is about to reverse, because rarely does a situation go in one direction indefinitely. The best low risk/high reward situations occur coming out of the turn. *A change in the direction of the discount rate has often signaled a major turn in the bond market and the stock market.*

INVEST WHEN THE CLIMATE OR CONDITIONS ARE FAVORABLE

When I was a young broker, I read that Jesse Livermore learned to buy only when the conditions were favorable. I had no idea what he was talking about. When I read where J. Paul Getty only invested when the climate was good, I had no idea what he was talking about. *Do you?*

Well, after twenty years plus of investing and speculating, I think I understand what they were talking about. *How I could have been so blind is embarrassing to me even now.* However, *that is part of the learning process,* I suppose. In any case, I am going to tell you what I think these men meant. *Please do not underestimate the value of this information.*

When interest rates have been high, and rising for sometime—say a year or two—*look for the first change in direction of the discount rate.* This has been the *key to many major turns in the market from a bear market to a bull market.*

Conversely, when a bull market has been raging for several years, watch out for the first change in the direction of the discount rate from down to up. This is an indication that the Federal Reserve Bank is taking the punch bowl away. The party is just about over; the music has stopped.

Ironically, it usually takes several increases in the discount rate to finally bring the bull market to its knees. In 1969–1970, there were five discount-rate increases; in 1973–1974, there were eight discount-rate increases; and in 1978–1979, there were thirteen discount rate increases.

A bear market, on the other hand, often ends abruptly, when the discount rate is cut; especially, if interest rates have been unusually high for a year or two. Once the rates start down, they tend to decline for two or three years or more.

THE OCTOBERS OF MY LIFE

Never go into October without a large cash position. Begin to reduce any margin debit by April and reach no debit by August, with cash being built from August into winter.

Major bottoms have occurred in October more often than most any other time. At major bottoms in the stock market, there are large numbers of stocks with P/E ratios of 10 and current ratios of 2:1. There were forty such stocks in 1974 and thirty-seven in 1980.

Tax-selling season is in full bloom during the October–December period. Most investors delay taking losses for as long as possible. Professionals take losses early, recognizing that the first loss is usually the smallest.

It seems that in October, the news media drags out the articles on the first stock market crash of 1929. This seems to stir up a decline. It has happened for many years. Why do the news people not drag out these programs in July, for instance? It seems that it is planned that way.

Why do so many important bottoms occur in October? I have heard different reasons, but none of them seemed to make that much sense to me. The liquidity of the banking system being strained the most at this period of time might be close to the best answer I have seen. However, just remembering the *dangers of October* should be enough to build you a small fortune in a reasonable period of time. I have devised a saying that might help you avoid the October declines. It goes like this:

> If you forget October in March, you will regret it in December.

Why? Because most of you will not take your losses until December, when the regrets come. March and April seem to see the tops of a lot of stocks each year. Therefore, remember to sell in March and April. Octobers have taken their toll on me over the years for not being aware of this information, which I now share with you. Upon reflection, an investor could literally buy in October–December and sell in March–April, and probably do better over the years than most any other method.

Therefore, tax selling, banking liquidity, and the winter blues make the Octobers a *weak period* for equity prices. *These are great months to buy* for those of you who remember to have cash available. *You must learn to buy low—in October through December—and sell high—in March through April.*

STOCK BUYING AND SELLING TENDENCIES

Stocks that are making lows now were making highs sometime in the past. Many stocks that are now down will be up another day. To buy quality stocks, when they are out of favor is to plant seeds for a bountiful harvest at a later date. The problem with most of us is: We want to see our stocks go up right after we buy them.

The really big moves I have seen usually take from one to three years and more. The percentage moves can be 300 percent, 400 percent, 500 percent, and I have seen stocks go up 1,000 percent and more in four or five years; from a major bear market bottom.

Patience is vital when you have a stock in a major uptrend. You must recognize that there will be reactions. Plan on them. If you know you are going to be scared during a sharp correction, then sell a portion on a spike up. Don't wait until you have had a 25 percent to 50 percent reaction to sell.

THE REVELATION OF MY LIFE

I have felt that self-confidence is extremely important in investing. I have placed my entire trading capital—my life's savings—in one stock position, more than once. I thought most investors could and would do the same thing.

Only in 1986 did I finally realize this cannot be done by most investors; nor should it be done by most investors. It is just that I had trouble realizing that most investors use the stock market as a hobby; not a full-time, all-or-nothing venture, as I do.

A neighbor, whom I had taught about investing, was at my home one night. I was discussing a forty-thousand-share position on the New York Stock Exchange that I had just liquidated. Bear in mind that this is a businessman who has considerable capital. He had a strange look on his flushed face. I asked, "What is wrong?" He said, "Don, you are really serious, aren't you?" "Sure," I said. "Why?"

"Don, I don't think you understand the average investor at all; and that is what I am. Sure, I have bought a thousand shares of the stock you showed me you had bought, but I had never owned more than a hundred shares of anything before I met you. You think everybody eats, drinks, and sleeps the stock market, Don; but I'm telling you—they don't."

It was then that *it hit me like a ton of bricks.* I had really grown up in the investment world; at least, I had grown from the young fellow who once traded two hundred or three hundred shares to a man who buys tens of thousands of shares. I had done it over twenty years. I never noticed the gradual change. *You can do it, too.*

PESSIMISTIC ARTICLES IN THE NEWS MEDIA

Watch out for pessimistic articles in newspapers by so-called experts, after a prolonged decline. This tends to accelerate the decline into a buying opportunity. At the very time when every fiber in your body says sell, make yourself buy. Just make sure the fundamentals for surviving are there.

Again, pay no attention to flattery from stockbrokers telling you how smart you are for having done this or that. They are interested in the commissions that will come from your account.

LEARN MORE AND MORE ABOUT LESS AND LESS

One of the secret keys to success in the stock market, commodity market, and most any endeavor in life is specialization. Learning more and more about less and less is very important. I have heard mediocre people say: "It's who you know that counts." I chose to acquire knowledge. I trust this approach more, in the long run, for I can depend on myself. As for others—and the market—I can depend on them to be devious and deadly. Knowledge is power!

I have dared to be independent and different. If you choose this avenue, make sure you understand the loneliness—before you try this route. No one will feel sorry for you, if you fail. In fact, there will be plenty who will laugh at you for thinking you could do it.

If you start such an endeavor, please remember the most important point, after you start, is . . . follow through.

ANSWERING MACHINE

Buy yourself an answering machine. They are cheap enough. They are excellent for screening calls. If you do not want to talk to someone, just ignore the call. It is rare, indeed, when someone is calling to stuff money into your jeans. If it is that great, they would be stuffing it into their jeans, not yours.

One young broker, to whom I had paid thousands of dollars in commissions, called me so much, I designed a letter, which you will find in this book (see p.2). I mailed it to all my stockbrokers, telling them never to call me again. When I visited the brokerage office again, later, the broker asked what he had done that angered me. I said, "If I knew as much about one thing, as you seem to know about so many things, I could make a million dollars in a hurry. Why is it, with all your knowledge, I am losing on every stock you have recommended?"

Never assume, because a broker has a fancy name or degree, that he can make substantial money in the marketplace. Commissions, yes, but that is not going to help you. I have known MBAs and PhDs who were terrible at investing for profits.

PATIENCE AND CONTROL OF YOUR EMOTIONS

Recessions come and go, and booms come and go. But the wise investor realizes that wealth can be built tremendously if he or she will wait for the pessimism to reach fever proportions, and sell when optimism is rampant. It takes about two years from the trough to the top, and about two years from the top back down into the trough. Emotions and markets rise and fall.

Not all stocks will follow this pattern exactly, but there is enough consistent repetition that you should be able to build a small fortune if you will study the lessons of the past. These patterns may not repeat exactly, but they are similar enough and often enough for a student of the market to recognize that *there is nothing really new in the marketplace*. Sure, the names change, but the game goes on and on. Politicians live and die. Investors live and die, but the market continues.

AUTOMATIC DIVIDEND PAYOUTS

Do not have your account put on automatic dividend payout. If the stock is held in your brokerage account in street name, just let the dividend hit the account. Then request a check or have it automatically put in a money-market fund so that it will start drawing interest immediately.

The day after the payable date, the dividend (or interest on a bond) should hit your brokerage account. I have received checks from brokerage firms as much as two weeks late when my account was on automatic-dividend payout. The postmark on the envelope would seem to be right, but three days in the mail from New York was standard for all my other mail. Why did it take two weeks for the checks to arrive from my brokerage account? Could it be that the firm was using my money for two weeks? If it was doing that with millions of dollars, then this is considerable interest income to the brokerage firm.

Note: Any time you delegate any of your rights away to someone with a conflict of interest, you had better prepare yourself to be abused. Where money is concerned, you should maintain tight controls. *Trust no one with your money.*

SYMPTOMS OF OVERCONFIDENCE*

1. Willingness to take larger than normal risks.
2. Accumulation of a much larger than average position in one market.
3. Accumulation of more than the usual number of positions in different markets.
4. General decline in adherence to trading rules.
5. Disregard of indications contrary to your present positions.
6. Willingness to ride losses longer than usual.
7. An increase in the "let's take a chance" type of attitude that accompanies rapid growth in profits.
8. Unwillingness to take profits at previously determined objectives.
9. A general euphoria and an accompanying belief that the best is yet to come.

*Reprinted by permission of the publisher from *The Investor's Quotient* by Jacob Bernstein (New York: John Wiley and Sons, Inc., 1980) 236–7.

SHORT-SALE VERSUS THE BOX

Do you have a substantial paper profit on stocks that you own? Would you like to move the gain into next year? A simple technique known as a *short-sale versus the box* might be just for you. It's really quite easy to do. There are arguments for and against this procedure. You should be the final judge of what is in your best interest.

Let's say you have five thousand shares of a stock and you have a short-term paper profit of $50,000. If you deposit your stock with a broker, you can instruct him to "sell short versus the box"—up to the number of shares you own—which is five thousand shares in this example.

The moment the transaction has been executed, several things happen. First, regardless of which way the stock fluctuates, there will be no effect on you, for you are long and short the same stock. You have locked in your profit which was your goal. You have also locked in the holding period; i.e., short-term or long-term, depending on the status of the position at the time of the transaction.

After the new year, simply call your broker and say: "Cross my long and short positions to close out the *short sale versus the box.*" Some brokers require instructions in writing. *Do this on the first day of business in the new year*—thus making your money available for other things. There should be no charge for closing this position out, since it is simply an accounting entry. Your funds should be available to you immediately.

One of the disadvantages of this technique is you lose the use of the money—in most cases—until the position is closed. Of course, while the money was invested in the stock, you were exposed to the ups and downs of the stock market—and your money was tied up then, also.

Another disadvantage is you will no longer get any dividends (should the stock pay a dividend) because any long-position dividend will be offset by a short-position dividend liability for the dividend. Again, this will be an accounting entry, i.e., debit versus credit.

You must consider your personal situation. Consult your tax adviser before doing anything. Also, shop around the different brokerage houses, both full-service and discount brokers, to see which one will offer you the best overall deal. There seems to be considerable differences in what the different firms will do for their clients on this particular transaction. There also seems to be considerable differences in commission charges. Remember, it is your money you are trying to protect.

Caution: Do not allow a stockbroker to liquidate one side of this position because it shows a substantial profit. Remember—the other side will be showing a similar loss. The broker may be looking at the commissions generated from the trades. *If you liquidate one side, you will have voided the original intent of the short-sale versus the box.*

Knowledge is power. Remember this technique.

AN EXAMPLE OF A HYPOTHETICAL CONVERTIBLE BOND

```
+------------------------------------------------------+
|    CONVERTIBLE    BOND           8% COUPON           |
|                                                      |
|                                                      |
|            +-----------------------------+           |
|            |    100 SHARES               |           |
|            |                             |           |
|            |    COMMON STOCK             |           |
|            |                             |           |
|            |                             |           |
|            +-----------------------------+           |
|                                                      |
|                                                      |
+------------------------------------------------------+
```

CONVERTIBLE BONDS—BONDS WITH STOCK BUILT INSIDE

The advantages of Convertible bonds are many.

Rule 1: You must like the company first. You must feel the common stock is going to appreciate in value sufficiently to warrant your buying into the company. This is what you do every time you buy common stock.

Rule 2: The premium you pay for the convertible bond over direct conversion should be no more than 10 percent to 15 percent. If the premium is more, you must like the company a great deal to buy it (the convertible bond). If the common stock pays no dividend, but is growing and the future looks bright, then you might pay the premium for the convertible bond; assuming the company had a convertible bond—which is not always the case.

Rule 3: The income (interest) on the convertible bond should be more than the dividend yield on the common stock.

Rule 4: Once the convertible bond trades below par (under $1,000), the downside price risk should be limited to the yield on the bond versus yields of other comparable bonds.

Rule 5: If the company is viable, the convertible bond represents an income vehicle with enormous upside potential, if the stock goes up substantially.

EXAMPLES OF HOW CONVERTIBLE BONDS MOVE

1. If the common stock were $10/share, the $1,000 bond would be about $1,000 plus a 10 percent to 15 percent premium, or $1,100 to $1,150.
2. If the common stock were $5/share, the convertible bond would usually stop declining as it went below par ($1,000) and the 8 percent coupon would cause the bond to perform as an income vehicle, not as a comon stock.
3. If the common stock were $15/share, there should be *no premium* (or very little) and the convertible bond should trade at direct conversion ($15 per share x 100 shares per bond = $1,500 per bond) in our example.

NOTE: Convertible bonds have the attraction of income usually higher than the common stock. The convertible bond tends to decline less if it is trading under direct conversion price, i.e., if the comon stock is under $10/share. It tends to trade at direct conversion once the common stock trades above $10/share in our example. The cost in commissions can be dramatically less in convertible bonds, but you must shop around. Discount brokers are usually more competitive than full-service brokers. Probably "all or none" orders should be used to avoid the minimum charge, when only a small part of an order might possibly be filled.

Convertible bonds are, often, used by smart corporate leaders to obtain free capital. Once the bond goes substantially above par (1,000), as the stock rises, the company can call the convertible bond; depending on the call features in the indenture, of course. Usually, the call price will be 105 ($1050) or so; about 5 percent above par. When an investor converts the inflated bond to stock, the only losers are, usually, the common stockholders and the convertible bondholders because their equity is being diluted by the conversion.

My advice to investors, usually, is to sell the convertible

bonds when they are called at substantial premiums and look elsewhere to reinvest their capital.

BUILDING A FORTUNE SYSTEMATICALLY

Ten thousand dollars can make you financially independent, if it is invested properly. Below is an example of how doubling $10,000 and deducting for taxes at a 28 percent rate can make you a fortune. However, you must reinvest the entire proceeds in order to achieve this goal. The average investor's lifetime can produce this result but you must understand what you are trying to achieve and stick with your goal. You will have to study and look for these opportunities. I have seen many such opportunities over the last twenty years.

MONEY	100 %	GROSS	28% TAX	NET
10,000	10,000	20,000	2,800	17,200
17,200	17,200	34,400	4,816	29,584
29,584	29,584	59,168	8,283	50,885
50,885	50,885	101,770	14,247	87,523
87,523	87,523	175,046	24,506	150,540
150,540	150,540	301,080	42,151	258,929
258,929	258,929	517,858	72,500	445,358
445,358	445,358	890,716	124,700	766,016
766,016	766,016	1,532,032	214,484	1,317,548
,317,548	1,317,548	2,635,096	368,913	2,266,183

Chapter 4

Long-Term Perspective (12–35 Years)—Study Groups, Then Individual Stocks

Study long-term charts of twelve to thirty-five years to get a sense of history. Securities Research Company of Boston, Massachusetts, provides the investor with excellent charts that cover this span of history in hundreds of companies.

Notice how there is a tendency of stocks to move up and down over time. Learn to study group behavior to help you spot future opportunities. Once a group moves in a particular direction, you can buy or sell most any stock within that industry and reap the benefits of the group tendency.

The following charts* are provided for examples only. No recommendations are made or implied.

*Charts courtesy of Securities Research Co., Babson-United Bldg., 101 Prescott St., Wellesley Hills, Massachusetts 02181-3319

DRUGS

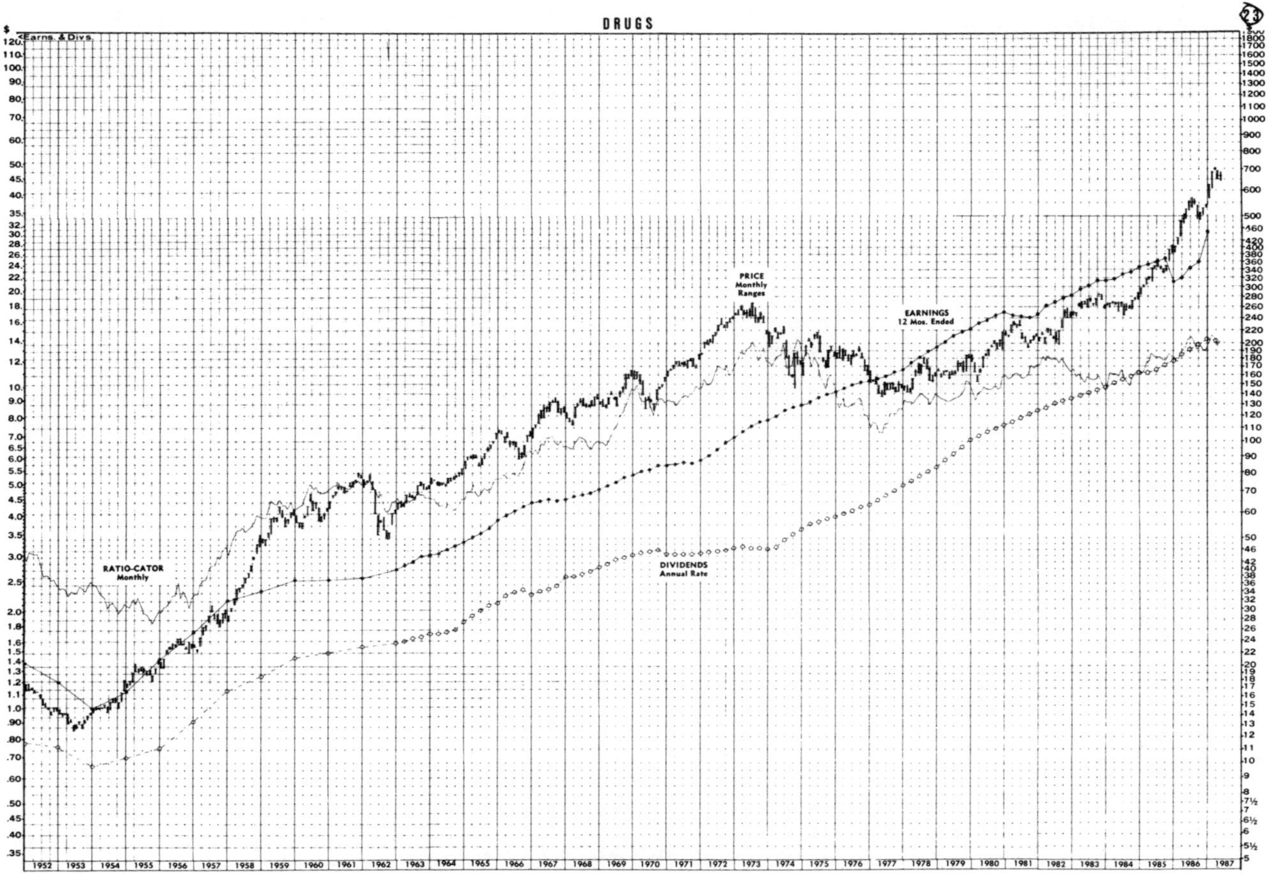
$ Earns. & Divs.
RATIO-CATOR Monthly
PRICE Monthly Ranges
EARNINGS 12 Mos. Ended
DIVIDENDS Annual Rate
1952 1953 1954 1955 1956 1957 1958 1959 1960 1961 1962 1963 1964 1965 1966 1967 1968 1969 1970 1971 1972 1973 1974 1975 1976 1977 1978 1979 1980 1981 1982 1983 1984 1985 1986 1987

MERCK & COMPANY, INCORPORATED (MRK)

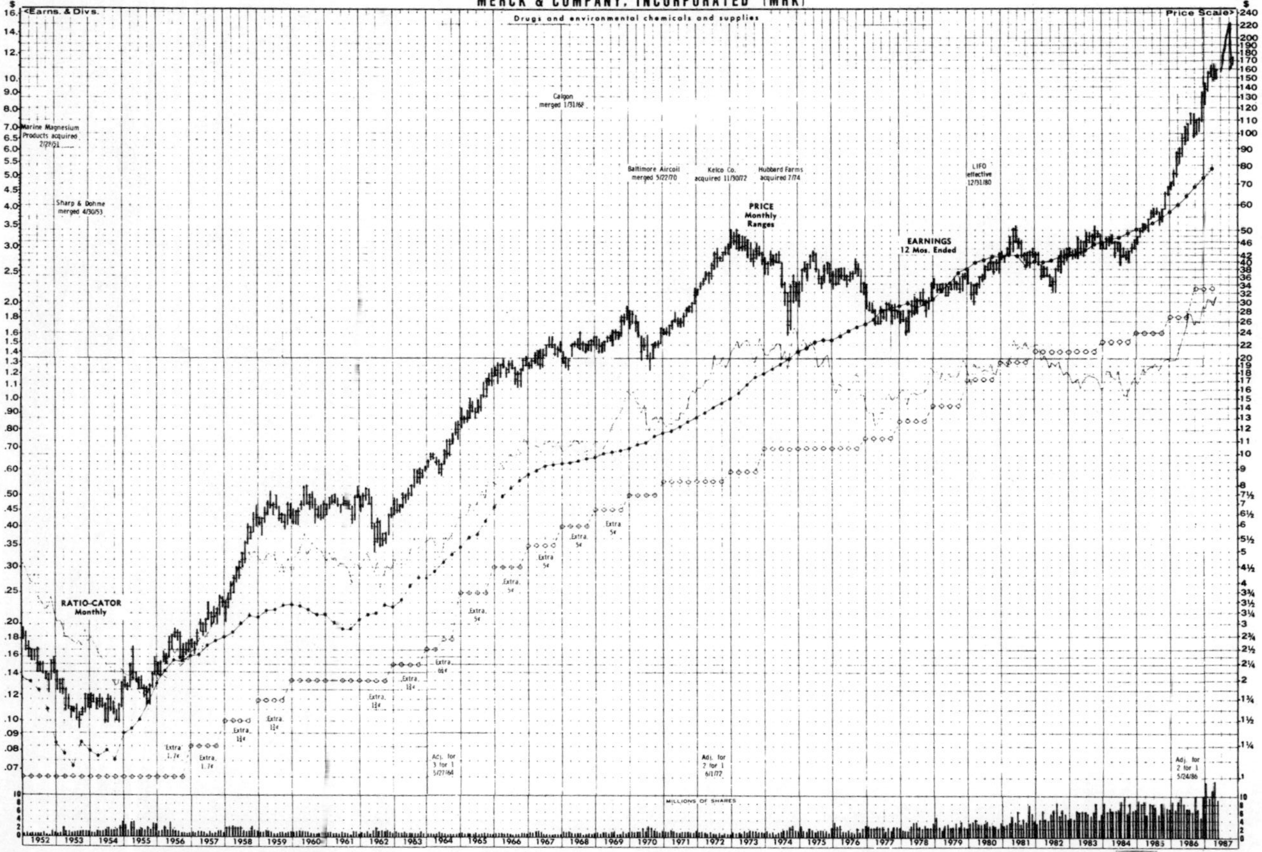

AUTOMOBILES

(13)

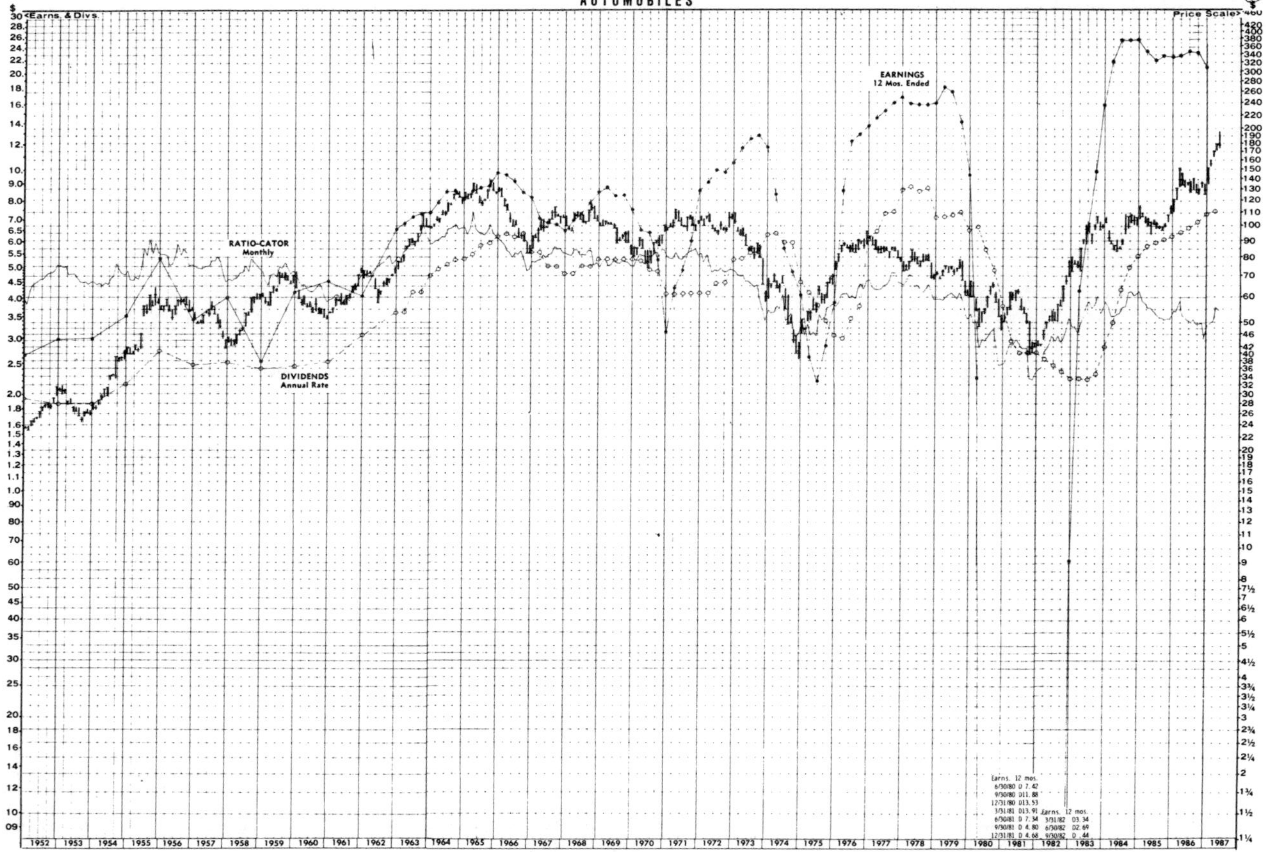

FORD MOTOR COMPANY (F)

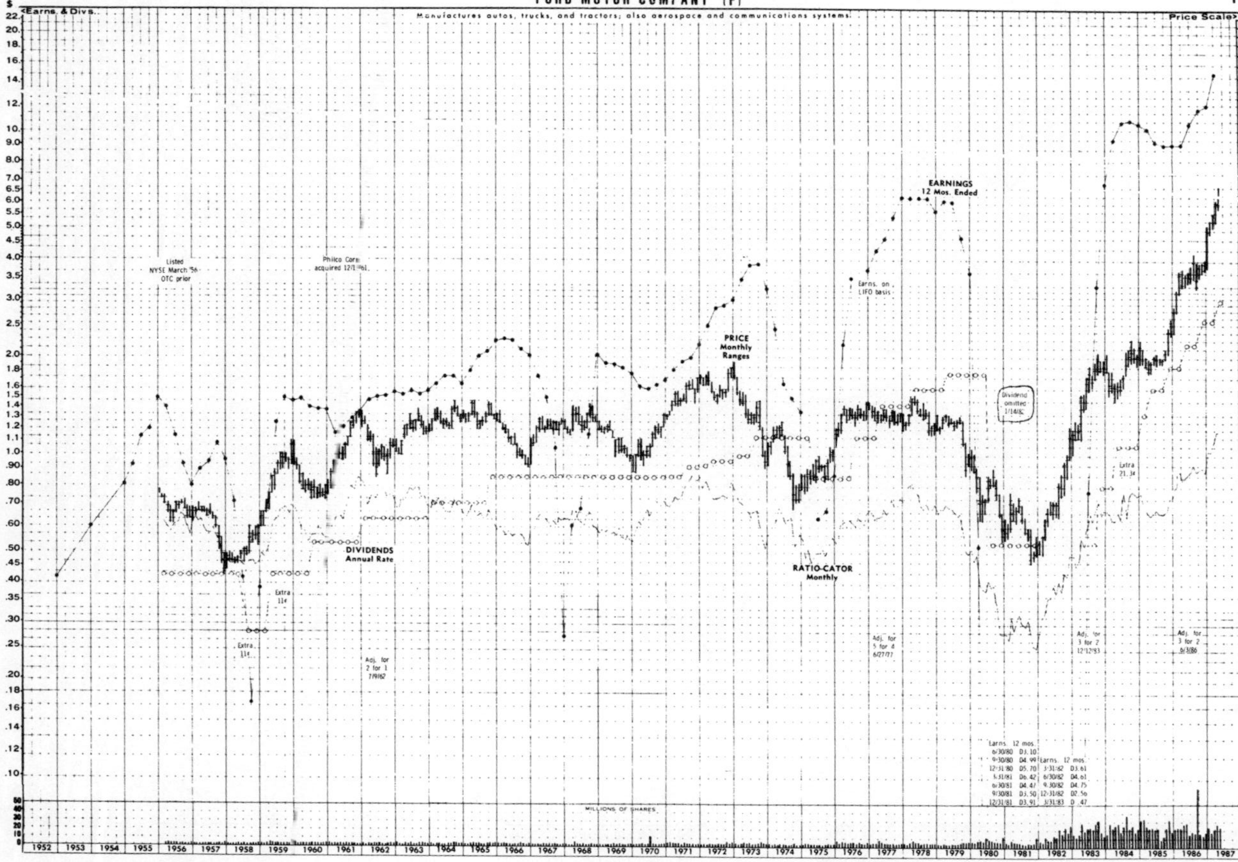

Chapter 5

Potpourri—Golden Nuggets of Information

POTPOURRI

DISCOUNT RATE: The stock market tends to rise for about thirty months after the low in the last discount rate cut. A rise of 15–50 percent in the averages after the low in the discount rate is typical. In other words, the top of the stock market could be seen about thirty months after the last discount rate cut.

—Wall Street saying

Speculating in the stock market is a *great deal* like *flying an airplane.* With limited (small) capital, you must keep your mistakes small. In a plane, a low altitude requires much care. As your altitude rises (more money), you have more cushion for error. However, the dangers are no less real.

—Donald E. Kendrick

Dream big dreams. If you aim for the stars and land on the moon, look how far you have still gone.

—Donald E. Kendrick

The men who can manage men manage the men who can manage only things, and the men who can manage money manage all.

—Will and Ariel Durant

Inflation—an elitist tool to get the rich, richer and make the poor, poorer.

—Unknown

I have learned to evaluate and judge a man by his consistent actions—not by his words.

—Donald E. Kendrick

The key to being a champion is consistency.

—Donald E. Kendrick

Historically, the spread between inflation and interest rates has been an average of 3 percent.

—Wall Street saying

Real power is not something someone gives you. You must learn to take and take.

—Donald E. Kendrick

Be like the duck; quiet and serene on top of the water, while paddling like crazy underneath.

—Wall Street saying

The long-term plan: The average investor must never forget his long-term plan. In the day-to-day activities, it is easy to forget; but you must not.

—Donald E. Kendrick

GOD to the technician is the *TREND.* Jesse Livermore discovered it and talked about it. Many have followed in his footsteps. No one seems to have come up with anything better.

—Donald E. Kendrick

Margin trading: I have had *many hundreds of thousands of dollars on margin* from time to time. I do not recommend using margin for most of you. Just as sure as night follows day, you will experience a big decline in your investment life. You will find out, very quickly, how margin can destroy you, if you are heavily margined and a huge sell-off comes in your stocks. Stockbrokers will not feel sorry for you. You borrow money from them to speculate; they want their money protected. They will sell your positions out, if they feel their capital is in danger. I would say about *margin trading: DON'T.*

—Donald E. Kendrick

Bears make their money quickly—when they are right. Optimists make their money slowly, over time—when they are right.

—Wall Street saying

When you find your blood pressure rising, be careful. Emotional decisions in the stock market are usually the worst kind.

—Donald E. Kendrick

Three phases of a bull market: interest rate rally, earnings rally, and foam—speculation.

—Wall Street saying

I have seen that trends tend to last for long periods, usually; more than weeks or months—often, for years. Interest rates, commodity prices, and stock prices tend to follow trends. This is where the fortunes are made; identifying the trend early and staying with it.

—Donald E. Kendrick

Bear markets tend to last about four hundred days or one and a half years. Bull markets tend to last about seven hundred days or two and a half years.

—Unknown

My greatest success has been achieved by doing business with brokers who kept their mouths shut or doing business with discount brokers; I prefer the latter.

—Donald E. Kendrick

No one said it was easy to make a million in the markets, but—I think—many people think it is. Therein lies a serious problem—and—DANGER!

—Donald E. Kendrick

People will believe a lie, if it is fantastic enough and told by a supersalesman.

—Unknown

I can depend on the stock market to be treacherous. So can you. People are like the stock market. A friend is an enemy that you cannot see because of your trust.

—Donald E. Kendrick

EARS = ENEMY
EYES = FRIEND

Good information needs to be seen, at the very least; not heard.

—Donald E. Kendrick

Declines: To assume that if the Dow-Jones is going to correct (move in the opposite direction to the major trend) 10 to 15 percent and that your individual stock will do likewise, is a very dangerous assumption—and, usually, wrong.

—Donald E. Kendrick

The first increase in interest rates usually does not kill a bull market. It takes time. But you should take that increase as a warning that the music is slowing down and you should look for a chair to sit in. Begin to move off the dance floor when you see the *first increase in the discount rate*. The music is about to stop, although it may be many months before it is obvious to the masses.

—Donald E. Kendrick

Some of my biggest winners were bought when they were down and dull, but the fundamentals were improving steadily. "Boring, boring, boring" were the words a stockbroker in Palm Beach, Florida, used to describe a stock in which I had forty thousand shares. *It doubled within twelve months.* I had twenty-three thousand shares of another stock. A stockbroker in another state said, "Don, your stock is so slow, it is like watching paint dry." I sold this stock for a *50 percent profit a short time later.*

—Donald E. Kendrick

Hope springs eternal; but never at bottoms.

—Unknown

The stock market hits bottom about four months before the economy hits bottom.

—Wall Street saying

Experience is a dear school, but fools will learn in no other. Most of the time they will never learn at all.

—Unknown

Scared at *bottoms; cocky* at *tops!* = The *average investor.*

—Donald E. Kendrick

If you have been successful in a bull market, be careful. You only find out how much you have learned when you keep what you have made, and not given it back in the next bear market.

—Unknown

One should never risk what one is not thoroughly prepared to do without. To be able to lose unemotionally is part of the key to being a big winner in most things in life. In the quest for gain, we too often forget how much we have to lose—until it is too late.

—Donald E. Kendrick

A winner must have the following: *Desire to win, will to win, and a killer instinct.*

—Donald E. Kendrick

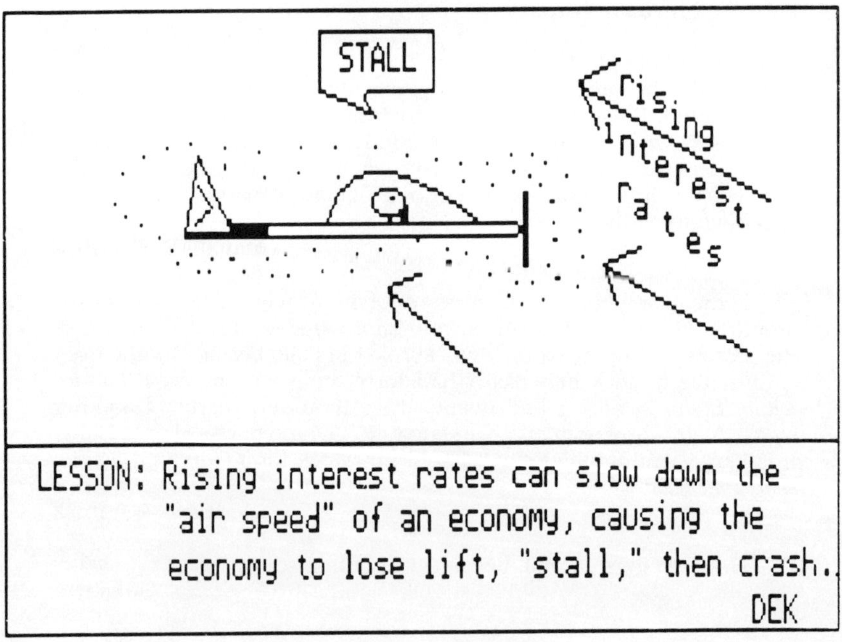

LESSON: Rising interest rates can slow down the "air speed" of an economy, causing the economy to lose lift, "stall," then crash.

DEK

As a pilot is landing an airplane, he pulls the nose up. The *stall warning buzzer* sounds to alert the pilot the *air speed* is insufficient to maintain lift. As the air speed continues to decline, the aircraft will, at some point, stop moving forward and drop. This is what happens at the point of landing, when the aircraft drops to the runway. Likewise, the stock market will begin to slow down as interest rates rise. The third increase in major interest rates usually is enough to do the trick. *The "stall" occurs! Down comes the market.*

—Donald E. Kendrick

I learned a long time ago that the best money to be made in the market consistently is to *look for stocks that have been knocked down from a past high price and the management has reduced debt, reduced cost, and made the company competitive.* Look for a trend in increased institutional holdings in shares. Earnings are not so important, initially, as they will follow, if the fundamentals are turning around.

—Donald E. Kendrick

Self-control is one of the main requirements to success in the stock market.

—Donald E. Kendrick

Some of the clues to finding a winner before the crowd on Wall Street:

1. Institutional holdings increasing.
2. A steep left wall as a result of a sharp decline in the stock.
3. Base building—one to five years.
4. Earnings increase even with a decline in sales.
5. Leader in its field.
6. Higher highs and higher lows in the stock price.
7. Dividend reinstatement or dividend increase.
8. Volume increases on rising prices; volume declines as prices decline.
9. Debt being reduced voluntarily.
10. Stock buyback to reduce outstanding shares.

—Donald E. Kendrick

Basic rule in stock investments: Equity prices are determined by the availability of cash to support those prices, i.e.:
high interest rates = low stock prices
low interest rates = high stock prices

—Donald E. Kendrick

When you are explaining to yourself why your stock is going down, you are losing.

—Donald E. Kendrick

When once a decision is reached and execution is the order of the day, dismiss absolutely all responsibility and care about the outcome.
—Prof. William James

Key to success: continuous, unyielding, overwhelming, persistent effort.

—Unknown

Opinions: So many investors have them, when so few are qualified to have them; stockbrokers, too.

—Donald E. Kendrick

Fear is quicker than greed, so the market drops faster than it rises.

—Unknown

What you tax, you get less of; what you subsidize, you get more of. If you tax investments and savings, you get less; if you subsidize welfare and unemployment, you get more.

—Unknown

A guarded tongue never speaks unwisely.

—Unknown

Give me the strength to face a fact, even though it slays me.

—Huxley

Doubt all before you believe anything.

—Sir Francis Bacon

Blind extrapolation of present trends with no regard for cycles is dangerous.

—Donald E. Kendrick

The really big fortunes have always been made on the long side of the market. From time to time, there are those who make it on the short side, but they are rare.

—Donald E. Kendrick

Knowledgeable people buy when the market is down and sell when the market is up. Therefore, look for strength in a down market and weakness in an up market. Of course, this is not perfect, as nothing is perfect. However, this is an excellent guide over time.

—Donald E. Kendrick

There are: 1) innovators, 2) imitators, and 3) incompetents.

—Unknown

Fear is not a good counselor.

—Donald E. Kendrick

Excellence, discipline, competence, and hard work make success.

—Coach "Bear" Bryant

I bet on the climate, which follows patterns, year after year, decade after decade . . . I've never been one to bet on the weather. It's unpredictable, changing from day to day.

—J. Paul Getty

Many men achieve success at different prices. Some pay at the cost of their health. Still others at the cost of their personal lives. But one price every man pays—the envy and jealousy of those he would have thought would have wished him well.

—Henry Flagler

It's sad when you can't trust anyone . . . ! It isn't sad; it's just one of life's most important rules . . . No more, no less!

—"Shogun"

Before you cross swords with someone:
1. Know you are right.
2. Have good reason to think you can win.
3. Make sure the reward is worth the battle.

—Donald E. Kendrick

Bear markets: The rallies are very sharp. The declines are slow, but relentless.
Bull markets: The rallies are slow. The declines are sharp.

—Wall Street saying

Bear markets: Three psychological phases:
1. The "awakening"—the shock after the speculative froth.
2. Stocks go down in response to obviously deteriorating business conditions.
3. Distress phase: Stocks sold for no other reason than to raise cash. Abandonment of hope, cash is king.

—Wall Street saying

That adversity which does not kill us, makes us stronger.

—Friedrich Nietzsche

You only have to "get rich" once; then, protect it.

—Donald E. Kendrick

A successful investor must learn to buy what is hated now; it can be loved later.

—Wall Street saying

The *sh-t sandwich:* The more bread (money) you have, the less *sh-t* you will have to eat.

—Wall Street saying

K.I.S.S.: Keep It Simple, Stupid.

—Wall Street saying

> Save as much as possible. Every person gets some luck in their lifetime, and the only reason most men never fulfill their business potential is they don't have the savings to take advantage of the luck when it comes along.
>
> —John Templeton

LOW PRICES ARE NOT NECESSARILY CHEAP PRICES

Remember, low is not, necessarily, cheap. Always look at the fundamentals of the company and the industry. Many stocks go down and end up bankrupt. Therefore, during panic days that are sure to come, look at values, as well as prices.

There is an old saying on Wall Street: "In a major decline, the good and the bad all go down. When better days come, the good go back up, and they haul the garbage off."

TOPS AND BOTTOMS

It is never standing-room only at the bottoms. It is usually very quiet in the average brokerage office around an important bottom. It is a time when many investors are sitting with big losses. It seems there can never be another bull (up) market. But, of course, in time, there will be.

At the top of the next bull market, the brokerage offices will be packed—standing-room only; very few will remember how depressed they were a few years earlier. And the beat goes on!

CHOICES WE HAVE

We don't get to choose what we are in life, when we are born. But we do have some choices as to what we become in life, after we are born.

Chapter 6

Securities and Exchange Commission (Suing Your Stockbroker after the Recent 1987 Supreme Court Ruling)—What Your Legal Rights Are

SUING YOUR STOCKBROKER

The Supreme Court of the United States says you can't sue your broker, if you have signed a binding arbitration agreement. So, do not sign the form.

The main complaints about stockbrokers I have heard are:

1. Churning an Account—Excessive buying and selling in an account with no regard for the objectives of the client.
2. Suitability—The needs of the client do not fit the investments purchased.
3. Unauthorized Trading—The stockbroker actually buys and sells in the account without the consent and knowledge of the client.
4. Fraud—This covers about everything, including taking money or securities out of the account.

The most important point you must always remember is this: If you see or suspect that something is wrong in your account, go immediately to the office manager. If your fears are not completely laid to rest, write immediately to the chairman of the board, and certify the letter with a return receipt requested. Recognize that managers have been known to be a part of a fraudulent scheme before, so do not put complete trust in this person either.

Also, recognize that the manager may stall for time, if there is a real problem with your account.

The letter to the chairman of the board will probably not get to him. However, you can bet it will get to the firm's legal council. He will, then, follow up on it *for the protection of the firm; not for your protection.* You will, in any case, get a definite response by taking this route. I know, for I have done this more than once.

You must remember that the local broker and the local manager do not want the higher-up executives to be bothered by local problems. Therefore, they will try to delay and postpone your answer, if there is a real problem. Do not delay. The primary rule in settling grievances of clients is: "React immediately; do not delay, for, to delay will be viewed as consent on your part." Ignore the patronizing words that you might get from the broker or manager. You are expected to watch out for yourself. If you do not, then do not expect mercy or kindness from Wall Street.

Suing your broker: It is almost impossible to sue your stockbroker, and win. Arbitration is your only way out at this time, and the cards are stacked against you, as far as I have been able to determine. When you sign an account form, you agree to binding arbitration in disagreements in many instances. The Supreme Court has recently ruled (1987) that arbitration should be used for claims under Section 10(b) of the 1934 Securities Exchange Act. This is the antifraud section, which is mostly used in complaints against stockbrokers. The kicker here is that claims settled by arbitration do not have to be made public, as a settlement in a court of law would be. So you see, you stand very little chance of total satisfaction when you get into trouble with a stockbroker. You certainly stand no chance in fighting the Supreme Court of the United States.

The *time to avoid these problems is at the very beginning. The less you trust your broker, the more likely you are to do well over your lifetime.* Your trust is better placed in your hands, if you can read, write, and think reasonably well. I know there are conscientious stockbrokers out there, who are trying to do a good job in a difficult environment. Their conflict of interest is simply tremendous.

"HOW TO TELL IF YOUR ACCOUNT IS BEING CHURNED"*

This article appeared in the September 1984 issue of *Futures* magazine, which is an excellent publication. The following list summarizes the main factors to be evaluated in determining churning charges against a broker:

1. Who is calling the shots in the account?
2. The customer's degree of sophistication and experience.
3. The customer's degree of trust placed in the broker.
4. The percentage of transactions the customer enters based on the broker's recommendations.
5. The customer's approval of recommended transactions where the approval was not based on complete, truthful, and accurate information supplied by the broker.
6. The absence of prior customer approval of transactions.
7. The amount of time the customer devotes to the account.
8. The nature and objectives of the customer's account.
9. The commissions generated by the account relative to the equity in the account.
10. The turnover rate.

LEGAL AND COMPLIANCE

Legal and compliance refers to the in-house inspections of stockbrokers. This is a joke as far as protection of the client is concerned. As many times as I had an inspection over eleven years, not once did anyone ask how profitable were the clients. It was usually a cursory glance at my holding pages. They seemed to be looking for concentrated positions in one stock. The entire procedure was a great big charade. With so much abuse going on, you would have thought some brokers would have been reprimanded. I never saw that—not even once.

*Reprinted by permission from *Futures* magazine, 219 Parkade, Cedar Falls, Iowa 50613.

LEGAL COMPLAINTS

If you ever complain about the activities of a stockbroker, you will find out why so few complaints are settled in favor of the client. Brokerage firms maintain a stable of attorneys who are well versed in defending their brokers and other personnel. You will find it almost impossible to reach a satisfactory conclusion if you have lost large sums of money. Rarely is a client made whole; i.e., gets all his money back.

The very best time to avoid this problem is in the beginning. Recognize that a salesman is not there to make you rich. He is there to sell you something; even the idea of trading, because that is where the commissions are. You only pay when you buy or sell, usually. Guard yourself against abuses in your acount. The best way, of course, is to make your own decisions and use a reputable discount broker.

If you wish to file a complaint with the Securities and Exchange Commission, I urge you to do so. Be sure and enclose all the facts, account numbers, and any pertinent information you have. The address is as follows:

Securities and Exchange Commission
Washington, D.C. 20549

YOUR LEGAL RIGHTS IN A BROKERAGE OFFICE

You have no legal right to be in a brokerage office. You are there by invitation. You are on private property. *You can be barred from a brokerage office by the manager in an instant.* It does not matter how many thousands of dollars in commissions or interest charges you have paid the broker. If the manager decides that you are a threat to his "kingdom," he can forbid you from ever entering his office again.

In discussing this matter with an attorney representing a major brokerage firm, the attorney stated that "clients are invited to enter the brokerage office. They are there by *invitation*. They are *permitted* to come on the premises. They do not have the right to be there, unless permission is granted."

The attorney added: "The manager of a brokerage office is chairman of the company in that location. Brokerage firms *choose to do business with whomever they wish.* A manager has the right to be *silly* over things if he or she wants to; if he or she feels like it. Things like *banning a client from his or her office* just because he does not want the client back in his office—is his right."

Brokerage firms do not have to explain why they do not want you back in their office. It is their private property. It is their right to do business with whomever they wish. Clients have no legal right to enter a brokerage office if that person is not invited. The client can be arrested for trespassing on private property if he is told to leave and does not. *It does not matter how much money you have paid them in commissions and interest charges. That counts for nothing.*

This was repeated so that you would realize the gravity of the situation. Remember this, the next time you are invited to buy or sell something from a broker.

LEGAL DEPARTMENT OF BROKERAGE FIRMS

Since I have seen some of these lawyers in action, I can state, categorically, that the average customer of a stockbroker has no chance at all in a battle with Wall Street attorneys. The killer instinct is the operative word with these individuals. You cannot imagine how ruthless some of these people can be. If you allow a stockbroker to churn your account into disaster, and, then expect to recover all your money, you are just dreaming.

The best time to avoid this problem is before you allow abuses to occur in your account. You must keep tight control over your assets, or you will lose them. If you try to make too much noise, the brokerage firm's attorney will tell you—straight out—that *they will sue you for defamation of the corporate name.* And, if you have any assets, you stand to lose them in a libel suit. I know, for I was told these very words. In other words, once you have allowed abuses to take place in your account, you will have great difficulties in getting them corrected—even partially.

Until you have tried to obtain restitution from a brokerage firm for abuses in your account, you have not really lived. Remember, the attorney representing the brokerage firm is not there to help you. He is there to protect the best interest of the firm paying him his salary. You are the enemy, in case you haven't figured that out yet. Their attorney is not interested in the truth; he is interested in protecting the firm that is paying him.

No matter how badly you have been abused and no matter how much money you have lost, you are the enemy. As for the stockbroker being your friend, just watch how quickly he hides behind the firm's legal department when difficulties arise. Watch the manager where your account was abused. He, too, will get behind the lawyers. I know for I have seen all of this happen in my eleven years as a stockbroker, as well as my twenty years plus around the investment community.

My advice, which I am repeating for it needs repeating, is to do business with a reputable discount broker. Make your own decisions. Believe me, it is not difficult. You will learn a great deal in the process. And, most important of all, you will not have that extra hand in your pocket all the time—plucking exorbitant commissions.

Chapter 7

Financial Publications that You Should Have

1. *Standard and Poor's Stock Guide* and *Bond Guide.*
   25 Broadway
   New York, New York 10004
2. *Wall Street Journal*
   200 Burnett Road
   Chicopee, Massachusetts 01020
3. *Barron's*
   200 Burnett Road
   Chicopee, Massachusetts 01020
4. *Futures*
   219 Parkade
   Cedar Falls, Iowa 50613
5. *Knight-Ridder Commodity Perspective*
   Desk Charts
   30 South Wacker Drive Suite 1820
   Chicago, Illinois 60606
6. Trendline's *Current Market Perspective*
   Trendline
   25 Broadway
   New York, New York 10004
7. Charts by Securities Research Co.
   101 Prescott Street
   Wellesley Hills, Maine 02181-3319
8. William O'Neil's *Daily Graphs*
   P.O. Box 24933
   Los Angeles, California 90024

Chapter 8

Tribute to Jesse L. Livermore

Reminiscences of a Stock Operator, by Edwin Lefevre, is truly a classic. If only I had discovered this book in my early years as a young stockbroker and speculator, I feel my path would not have been so bumpy.

You would do well to buy this book and read it often. If you buy and sell any financial instrument, this book will help you—*for the rest of your life.*

It is my understanding that Jesse Livermore actually penned this book; he wanted to remain anonymous at the time the book was written. Every speculator or investor who has read this book has benefited greatly. For an individual to write such a book, to try to assist other speculators, is a credit to that individual.

Jesse Livermore was, in my opinion, one of the truly great innovators in the world of speculation. His discoveries about trends and human emotions within the stock and commodity markets have been used over and over by traders and investors throughout the world. Mr. Livermore's discoveries have stood the test of time. That is the mark of a brilliant man. Mr. Livermore also wrote a fascinating book titled *How to Trade in Stocks.*

Both of his books can be purchased at the following two publishers for anyone interested:

1. Fraser Publishing, Box 484, Burlington, Vt. 05402
2. Traders Press, Box 10344, Greenville, S.C. 29603

The following extracts are from *Reminiscences of a Stock Operator:*

> . . . The trader must look far ahead, but the broker is concerned with getting commissions now; hence, the inescapable fallacy of the average market letter. Brokers make their living out of commissions from the public. (p. 15)

The speculator's deadly enemies are ignorance, greed, fear, and hope. All the statute books in the world and all the rules of all the Exchanges on earth cannot eliminate these from the human animal. (p. 286)

It has always seemed to me the height of damnfoolishness to trade on tips. I suppose I am not built the way a tip-taker is. I sometimes think that tip-takers are like drunkards. There are some who can't resist the craving and always look forward to those jags which they consider indispensable to their happiness. It is so easy to open your ears and let the tip in. (p. 202)

The sucker has always tried to get something for nothing and the appeal in all booms is always, frankly, to the gambling instinct aroused by cupidity and spurred by a pervasive prosperity. People who look for easy money invariably pay for the privilege of proving conclusively that it cannot be found on this sordid earth. (p. 234)

The following extracts are from *How to Trade in Stocks:*

The lesson here again is that speculation itself is a business and should be so viewed by all. Do not permit yourself to be influenced by excitement, flattery or temptation. Keep in mind that brokers sometimes innocently become the undoing of many speculators. Brokers are in the business to make commissions; they cannot make commissions unless customers trade. The more trade, the more commissions. The speculator wants to trade and the broker not only is willing but too often encourages over-trading. The uninformed speculator regards the broker as his friend and is soon over-trading. (p. 42)

One major mistake of all speculators is the urge to enrich themselves in too short a time. Instead of taking two or three years to make 500% on their capital, they try to do it in two or three months. (p. 39)

Chapter 9

Acknowledgments

1. *The SRC Green Book of 5-Trend 35-Year Charts, 1952–1987,* © 1987, Securities Research Co., Babson-United Bldg., 101 Prescott Street, Wellesley Hills, Massachusetts 02181.

2. *Contrarian Investment Strategy: The Psychology of Stock Market Success* by David Dreman, © 1979, Random House, E. 50th Street, New York, New York 10022.

3. *Cycles: The Science of Prediction* by Edward R. Dewey and Edwin F. Dakin, © 1947, Henry Holt & Co., New York, New York 10175.

4. *Economic Meteorology X* by Morgan Maxfield, © 1977, National Youth Foundation, 2918 Commerce Tower, Kansas City, Missouri 64105.

5. "The 40 Month Cycle in Stock Prices" by Gertrude Shirk, *Cycles,* November 1982, Foundation for the Study of Cycles, 125 S. Highland Avenue, Pittsburgh, Pennsylvania 15206-3979.

6. *How I Made $2,000,000 in the Stock Market* by Nicolas Darvas, © 1960, Lyle Stuart, Inc., 120 Enterprise Avenue, Secaucus, New Jersey 07094.

7. *How the Average Investor Can Use Technical Analysis for Stock Profits* by James Dines, © 1972, Dines Chart Corp., P. O. Box 22, Belvedere, California 94920.

8. "How to Tell If Your Account Is Being Churned" by H. Richard Mayberry and Felix Rosenthal, *Futures,* September 1984, Merrill J. Oster, 219 Parkade, Cedar Falls, Iowa 50613.

9. *How to Trade in Stocks* by Jesse Livermore, © 1966, Investor's Press, Inc., Palisades Park, New Jersey 07650.

10. *Investor's Quotient: The Psychology of Successful Investing in Commodities and Stocks* by Jacob Bernstein, © 1980, John Wiley & Sons, Inc., New York, New York 10158.

11. *Jesse Livermore: Speculator-King* by Paul Sarnoff, © 1967, Investor's Press, Inc., Palisades Park, New Jersey 07650.

12. "Making Democracy Less Inflation-Prone" by Robert Lubar, *Fortune Magazine,* September 22, 1980, Time, Inc., Alexandria, Virginia 22314. All rights reserved.

13. Muriel Siebert & Co., 444 Madison Avenue, New York, New York 10022.

14. *Reminiscences of a Stock Operator* by Edwin Lefevre, © 1982, Fraser Publishing, Box 494, Burlington, Vermont 05402.

15. *Scientific Stock Speculation* by Charles H. Dow, © 1920, Windsor Books, Brightwaters, New York 11718.

16. *The Professional Commodity Trader* by Stanley Kroll, © 1985, Traders Press, Inc., Box 10344, Greenville, South Carolina 29603.

17. *Viewpoints of a Commodity Trader* by Roy W. Longstreet, © 1969, Frederick Fell, Inc., New York, New York.

18. *Wall Street Journal,* Dow-Jones & Co., 200 Burnett Road, Chicopee, Massachusetts 01020.

19. *Why Most Investors Are Mostly Wrong Most of the Time* by William X. Schienman, © 1970, Weybright and Talley, 750 Third Avenue, New York, New York 10017.